Laughing Through Life

Connie Corcoran Wilson

LAUGHING THROUGH LIFE

by

Connie (Corcoran) Wilson

Quad City Press 2011

Humorous essays that appeared in a variety of online and print journals, including " Metro East," "The Rock Island Reminder," "www.WeeklyWilson.com" and "www.BlogforIowa.com"

www.WeeklyWilson.com

www.ConnieCWilson.com

For information, address:

Quad City Press

2127 3rd St. B

East Moline, IL 61244-2409

www.EINNOC10@Aol.com

Published in the USA by Quad City Press, Inc.

ISBN—978-0-9824448-3-2

Contents

ESP: Exercise in Stress Points

I have devised a point system similar to that scale used to tell when a person has too much stress in his or her life. My scale is designed to warn you when you have signed up for an exercise class that is too difficult for you.

On the life stress scale, a marriage, divorce, new baby or death in the family might equal 100 points. On my exercise stress point scale, you are assigned Exercise Stress Points (ESP) to signal when you are in a world of hurt.

For openers, you can always tell you're in serious trouble if you are the only one who looks like they really *need* the class and are the only one not wearing leg warmers. After that, the scale is as follows:

10 ESP (exercise stress points): Class assembles. Instructor leads vigorous calisthenics for a full twenty minutes. You are exhausted and turning blue. Just as you are about to collapse quietly in a corner, your group leader—who always has a name like Bambi or Heidi—chirps, "Now that we're all warmed up, let's begin our first set of exercises." This question flashes through your mind: when, exactly, did *her* exercises become *our* exercises?

20 ESP: You discover that the rest of the class has been working out at home to Jane Fonda's Advanced Exercise tape. You have been

using a Debbie Reynolds record and "Sweatin' to the Oldies." Add five more ESP if you think Richard Simmons is "cute."

30 ESP: Your pants split up the back as you attempt to do a backwards roll.

40 ESP: Woman next to you on your left looks at your beet-red face and comments, "I see you're flirting with Old Mr. Blood Pressure."

50 ESP: When you are supposed to check your pulse to see if you have achieved your level of aerobic fitness, you cannot find yours. No one else can, either. You hope this does not mean that you have been declared legally dead at some point during the last twenty minutes.

60 ESP: You begin to hyper-ventilate and are forced to put your head between your legs—no easy task! Later, it takes two class members to remove your head from between your legs.

70 ESP: Food fantasies occupy your thoughts. Complete this sentence, "Gee, after all this, I can go up to Hagen Daaz and......" "Jog around the block" is not the phrase you would use to complete this sentence.

80 ESP: Woman on your right, having made contact with the funny bone in your right elbow with her exercise wand, says, "Excuse me. I'm a little out of practice. I just got out of the hospital yesterday; the quints are doing fine!"

As the pain escalates, you try to decide whether to (A) steal her exercise wand after class and burn it as an offering to the Exercise God (if She exists), or (B) grab it out of her hand RIGHT NOW and break it over your knee. You opt for (B), grabbing and breaking.

90 ESP: You are ejected from the class and the club for willfully and wantonly destroying another class member's exercise wand. As you leave, with your pants gaping wide, you are heard muttering about the population explosion.

100 ESP: Your husband hits the roof. He discovers that your $500 health club membership fee is non-refundable once you have begun class AND you are billed $50 for the broken exercise wand!

For Bad Luck, Bigger is Better

The carpet man came to replace my blue bathroom carpeting yesterday. The old carpeting was only two years old. It was barely worn and matched the wallpaper—and had a burned spot the size of a dinner plate precisely in the middle!

All this came about when my handy dandy space heater shorted out just as I was about to step into the tub. Since I wasn't exactly dressed in my Smokey the Bear fire-fighting costume at bath-time and had no desire to ruin any good towels by putting a fire out with them, I quickly unplugged the heater, crouched on my hands and knees, and blew the flames out.

A charming sight, I assure you.

Two days before the carpetman was due to replace the burned blue carpeting, it rained in the night and flooded the basement bathroom, recently re-decorated in shades of orange.

So, while the carpet man was here repairing the burned blue carpeting, I asked him to take a look at the flooded orange carpeting. If it's not fire, it's flood.

"Geez, lady!" he hollered up from the basement," You've got a regular swamp down here! Have you contacted your insurance man?"

I dialed our insurance man, Alibi Ike. He informed me that the next time I set fire to the bathroom, "You should really torch it out!" It seems that we have a $250 deductible on our insurance policy. The total repair bill was $236.74.

Ike, the insurance man, never a quick study, intoned, "Now…let me get this straight. You were struck by lightning?"

"Uh….no, Ike," I answered. "The lightning woke me up. It was rain or hail that did the damage. You can see the water marks on the window of the basement bathroom window well."

"Oh, gee. We don't cover water damage."

"Let me see if I have this right. You don't cover fire damage. You don't cover water damage. Just exactly what DOES this insurance cover, Ike, because I'd like to get some good out of it?"

"I hear you! I hear you! Did you say that there was hail damage?"

"I didn't, but I *can* , Ike. Would that help? Tell them it hailed on the carpet and dented it. Tell them anything you want, Ike, but get me some good out of this policy!" I hung up, feeling frustrated.

Just as I was feeling my most thwarted, news came of a woman who was driving oh-so-very-carefully across some bumpy railroad tracks one recent day, in an attempt to keep the undercarriage of the family roadster in one piece.

Naturally, she had all the kids in the car, and, since she was being *very* careful not to hit any of the bumps too hard, she became stuck right in the middle of the tracks, just as a train approached.

She and I have to look on the bright side. I didn't burn the house down; she managed to get the kids out of the car right before the train totaled it.

Sometimes, bigger is better, like when you want try to file an insurance claim, apparently, but sometimes you just have to make peace with your situation and move on.

To the Victims Go the Spoils

I found something that resembled grass in my refrigerator drawer this morning. It was either very moldy bacon or badly decomposed celery—take your pick. Even though it had an obnoxious odor and the consistency of slime, it wasn't nearly as odious as some of the things I save only to find them later—*much* later!

As one frequent dinner guest, a bachelor, said to me recently, "Oh, what the heck! I'll throw caution to the winds! Pass the salad dressing!"

I reminded him of two old sayings, "Beggars can't be choosers," and "The price is right."

He countered with his own saying: "To the victims go the spoils."

Citrus fruit seems to have a special affinity for going gray-green in my kitchen. Self-respecting oranges, like elephants, pick a spot to die: my hydrator drawer. Alexander Fleming, discoverer of penicillin, would think he had discovered the Mother Lode.

Grapefruit fare no better. Once a grapefruit, always a grapefruit. Unless it's a grapefruit in my refrigerator. I've tried passing them off as fuzzy shrunken basketballs for pygmies, but my family knows a decaying grapefruit when they smell one. They have a well-developed sixth sense about such things.

It is a well-known fact that Alexander Fleming accidentally discovered penicillin when he noticed a bit of mold had fallen from a culture plate in his laboratory and had destroyed bacteria around it. Less well-known is the fact that Fleming also discovered lysozyme, a substance found in human tears.

There is no truth to the rumor that Fleming discovered both while rutting around in my refrigerator on defrosting day.

Kroehler's Secret

A young single girlfriend with the unusual first name of Pan stayed overnight with me in Iowa City at the time I was taking the State of Iowa Writers' Workshop two-week course. You should have heard me encouraging her visit.

"Come on up, Pan. Seriously! There'll be lots of single guys for you! The place'll be lousy with them! You'll love it! You can sleep on the hide-a-bed in my apartment. I'll take you out for dinner. I know a place where they have terrific food!"

When she arrived, tired from her long drive from the Twin Cities, she asked if she could take a short nap before dinner.

"Sure! No problem! It's nice and quiet around here."

Unfortunately, the neighbors were felling a tree directly outside my bedroom window.

Dinner held no more luck for my visitor. The Chinese dish that Pan ordered from the menu at the restaurant was so bad the manager approached us, unbidden, asking, "How's your dinner?"

She reluctantly admitted that it tasted as though an entire bottle of soy sauce had been dumped in just one serving.

"We've had several complaints about it. It must be the new brand of soy sauce. We aren't serving it any more and would like to replace your meal."

After dinner, we discovered that Maxwell's and the Field House, two well-known Iowa City watering holes, were locked and dark. In our neighborhood on the way home, we couldn't even find a place to buy a cup of coffee—and it was only 10:30 p.m.

We tried Wendy's, a pizza place, and a bowling alley before we went to a grocery store and bought instant coffee to make back at my apartment.

When Pan and I tried to open the hide-a-bed she would be sleeping on, there was a little tag attached that said: "Kroehler—the couch with a secret."

The secret—which is still safe with Kroehler—was how to open the hide-a-bed!

There was one bright spot for a single girl during the evening, though. We did find a males-only convention in progress at our restaurant.

It was a convention of priests.

Number 401, Vincent Van Gogh, and Me

Today, I had my ears pierced. It's something I've been building up the courage to do for more than a decade. I think of it as a symbolic act, a statement of my independence and maturity. My mother always disapproved of pierced ears in her own inimitable fashion and felt they were somehow "cheap" and vaguely gypsy-like.

I, on the other hand, had come to feel that all the truly smart, chic, uptown and stylish women had pierced ears. There was no room for compromise. I felt the way I did about going down Space Mountain at Disneyworld. I knew it was something I should do because it was supposed to be GREAT, but I also knew that I threw up after my last ride on the Tilt-a-Whirl. Hardly a recommendation for future rides. Never one to give in easily to peer pressure, I felt apprehensive and anxious. People who tried to allay my fears made me feel worse.

So, today, I went about deciding whether to pierce my ears very scientifically.

I flipped a coin.

Heads, I did it. Tails, I did not.

It came up heads. My teen-aged son and I went back to the boutique advertising this special.

"Don't you want to go play video games?" I asked son Scott, whose eyes are permanently glazed from such activity.

"No. I want to watch."

The young clerk—Kathy by name—seemed quite knowledgeable. No, the posts did not have to be 14K gold these days. These were surgical steel and would work just as well. They were hypo-allergenic.

By this time, I was hyper-aller-nauseous.

After she had assured me that she had done over 400 people and had personally trained all her girls, I submitted, on condition that the store manager Kathy, herself, and one of her two young assistants, administer the coup de grace.

"Just what I need," I thought, "two more holes in my head."

Kathy carefully positioned me on the stool, explaining that, since I was obviously apprehensive (read: scared out of my mind) I should sit down so that I wouldn't fall down and hurt myself if I fainted.

That is somehow not a very reassuring statement at such moments.

This was followed by, "It would have been good for you to have brought another adult."

Hmmmmmm. Ominous.

I sat. She grabbed her trusty staple gun. I began verbally rattling aloud like a Chatty Cathy doll, figuring the date it would be when my six weeks of post-twirling and sterilizing would be up.

Six people had gathered to watch: two women, obviously as nervous as I, and three sober wide-eyed girls in their teens. And, of course, my first-born.

Kathy, in a voice like kindly old Doc Welby soothing a hysterical patient, said, "Now you're going to hear a loud click." I was glad that she hadn't said, "Now you are going to hear a LOUD boom."

I only heard a soft click above my nervous nattering and calculating.

Then I heard Kathy say, "Oh oh. This has never happened to me before. It didn't go all the way through."

Who knew I had the world's thickest ear lobes? I knew that 401 was not destined to be my lucky number.

I suggested to Kathy, who was, by now, sweating profusely, "You might as well go through with fixing it, Kathy. It's a little like childbirth. It's kind of hard to go back now! You know what I mean?" This brought a chuckle from the assembled crowd. Then, with a flash of inspiration fueled by fear, I said, "Of course, we could just hang a matching staple gun from my left ear and try to start a new fad."

The shop girls tried unsuccessfully to suppress their laughter.

I noticed that Kathy, who was sawing determinedly at the post and gun in my ear, did not laugh. She was muttering softly to herself. Something about being warned there'd be days like this, but why did they have to happen to her?

My ear was now the consistency and color of chopped liver, and I was trying that old dentist's chair stand-by: alternative pain to distract. There is no end to this story. Kathy put the left ear post in without incident, and I left, telling her that it was probably not her fault. Although, in these situations, whose fault is it, really?All three of the adult onlookers fled, although one of them ventured the opinion that I should have been given a free pair of earrings. Or ears. Whichever would be cheapest and easiest.

Kathy pretended not to hear that crack, just as she had pretended not to hear the suppressed laughter of her staff.

So, for a mere $10, I got a cauliflower ear and instant empathy with one of history's greats: Vincent Van Gogh.

Number 401, Vincent Van Gogh, and me.

Ten Rules to Remember When You Entertain

The following are Wilson's Ten Rules of Entertaining, or how to eat your heart out:

RULE 1: The number of guests shall always be one more than the number of matching plates.

RULE 2: The guests, when they equal the number of available matching cups or glasses, will misplace their cup and/or glass, requiring that a Jolly Olly Orange mug or a glass bearing a facsimile of either Porky Pig or Daffy Duck be pressed into service.

RULE 3: If all the guests arrive, the pre-ordered hors d'oeuvres won't.

RULE 4: Gravy made for company will always either separate or have lumps.

RULE 5: The most important guest at a dinner party will always receive the chipped cup (every dinner service has one), no matter how carefully the hostess sets the table.

RULE 6: Chairs will mysteriously disappear just when they are needed most.

RULE 7: At least one guest will be allergic to whatever you serve; one will have a rare swallowing disorder that makes it necessary to have bland pablum, rather than the main entrée; and a whopping fifty per cent will be on strict diets.

RULE 8: Whatever is supposed to rise will fall, and whatever is supposed to fall will rise. This can be summarized as, "What goes up must come down—but please not until I've served the soufflé!"

RULE 9: Whatever the recipe calls for, you won't have it on hand. If you think you do have it on hand, you will discover at the last moment that the container is empty. The only convenience store open at this time of the evening will not have whatever it is.

RULE 10: If anything can be spoiled, dropped, burned, or lost, it will be if the event is an important dinner party. Conversely, perfect meals are the order of the day when only your own immediate family or people you hate are being served.

One restaurant actually *lost* a five-foot sandwich I had ordered for a party. How do you "lose" a five-foot sandwich?

There are several corollaries that accompany Wilson's Rules of Entertaining, which will be left for later. Among these are: never serve anything that was not green when you purchased it or moves when you open the box; don't throw oil on troubled waters or water on oil fires; and save the family photo album in the event of a kitchen three-alarmer. The closest we came to a three-alarm fire was the memorable pretzel-in-white-chocolate dipping party, which nearly resulted in third degree burns when Number One son caught the waxed paper on fire. He was oblivious. The flames were climbing up the waxed paper towards his arm while I stared, mesmerized. Somehow, I managed to grab his arm and the fork that had the waxed paper (which had adhered to the pretzel), still blazing, attached, and throw it (the fork, not the arm) in the sink. We later learned that his uncle, for whom we were making this delicacy as a Christmas present, hated white chocolate pretzels because he had once eaten an entire box by himself and became violently ill immediately thereafter. He thought it was some kind of cruel joke at his expense.

And you always thought the phrase, "Dinner will be ready when the smoke alarm goes off!" was a joke.

My Most Memorable Dinner Party

I once invited four couples for a dinner that turned out to be doomed. It was, quite literally, the dinner party from hell!

It was near Thanksgiving, and I always make a twenty-pound bird for the entire family at Thanksgiving. From having done this every year since 1968, I have, imbedded in my admittedly lame memory bank, the information that turkeys take "twenty minutes to the pound." Who needs to look up stuff you already "know?" However, I was planning to use our new microwave to fix a turkey breast, and, of course, in the microwave, it takes much, much less time. I found this out the hard way.

I put the turkey breast in the microwave and set it for the appropriate amount of time *for the conventional oven.* Who knows how long that was? One hour? Two hours? Then, I went back to my hostessing chores, which consisted largely of drinking wine in a separate room off the kitchen and conversing with my guests.

When the smoke alarm went off, I discovered that there was a football-shaped object in my microwave that was completely black and charred. It was smoking.

I tried, delicately, to get my husband to join me in the kitchen, so that we could discuss this problem. He, of course, was oblivious, having *really* gotten in to helping me with my hostessing chores, i.e., drinking.

Finally, he came to the kitchen only to agree with me that the turkey was a goner.

I sent him out for Colonel Sanders' chicken, which, conveniently, went with everything else we were having (stuffing, scalloped corn, mashed potatoes, etc.)

As we gathered to pass the bucket and chow down, a mouse ran through my dining area, immediately under the large round oak table at which we were seated. Every woman in the place screamed, and, like the June Taylor Dancers on crack, jumped, in unison, onto their chair seats.

People still mention this dinner party to me. I don't know why.

I tell them that my father, years earlier, had predicted a bright future for me in the kitchen. I left a light-weight aluminum pan on an electric stove burner and left to go swimming. As I recall, this large pot had some water in it at some point. Obviously, I did not realize that I had left the burner on to depart for several hours of swimming.

When I returned home, all the windows in our kitchen were out….I mean OUT. Literally. The glass was gone and smoke was pouring from the windows and firemen were present. The water in the pan had boiled dry and then the aluminum pan apparently melted and, drop by aluminum drop, dripped into the innards of our electric stove.

My father took the cooled fifty-cent sized piece of aluminum and drilled a hole in it and gave it to me, saying, "Whoever gets you for a wife is going to really have their work cut out for them, since you can't even boil water." He said this with a smile, I think, glad that I had not set the entire house on fire.

I am a pretty good cook today, but I can't promise anything, as far as the long-term damage to the kitchen.

A Sole in Distress

I have a lot of trouble with shoes. You might say that, over the years, more than once I have been "a sole in distress."

My mother constantly chided me, in my youth, to buy "sensible shoes." What are "sensible shoes?" Shoes are inanimate objects; I never expected them to make sense. I never spent long hours locked in dialogue with my sneakers. There have been times, though, that I have directed some harsh remarks to an offending pair.

For example, there was the time in the sixties, in college, when I got the three-inch spike heel of my black suede pumps caught in a street grating while walking to church. For a short period, I imagined myself entering church barefoot or wearing a 4-foot square grill attached to my left heel. There was the time that my toddler son got his foot firmly wedged in the supermarket cart undercarriage. Never one to do things the easy way, I laid the cart on its side in the supermarket aisle to dislodge it. Later, it occurred to me that I could have simply had him slip his foot from the shoe, but, by then, I had chosen the less efficient method and a crowd had gathered. Once, while at a discotheque dancing, the strap on a pair of black patent leather flats broke. I learned that it is impossible to safety pin the strap and continue dancing using this repair technique.

Perhaps the most unusual episode, until now, was the New Year's Eve that television star Vicki Lawrence's mother tried to buy the fancy dress shoes I was wearing right off my feet at Lawry's, the famous Los Angeles eatery. It was weird and had something to do with them being a 7AAA, which isn't even my size. I had kicked them off while waiting for hours, and, when I went to retrieve them, Mrs. Lawrence was on the banquette in front of the glitzy shoes and noticed the odd size, which was, apparently, hers, even if it wasn't mine. I don't know why I bought 7AAA shoes when my true size was 5 and ½ "B" width. They were there. I liked them. It defies logic, as all my shoes purchases do. They were the Everest of shoes.

While in Hawaii over Easter break we went to see Bill Cosby perform at the Maui Hyatt. In order to get to the concert, we had to park about a mile away on a golf course and walk in through a back door. While we were crossing the golf course, the automatic sprinkler system kicked in, thoroughly soaking the grass and us. Coincidentally, this final day of our trip, confident that we had somehow avoided the sun god's wrath for the prior eight days, all three of us had sustained serious sunburns. The tops of my feet were beet red, and nylons were out of the question. In fact, the only shoes that I could tolerate, at all, on my red, swollen ankles, were a pair of soft cloth slings which were, figuratively and literally, on their last legs.

After we hit the golf course sprinkler system…or it hit us….one shoe kissed its sole goodbye. The top of the shoe was attached at the heel only, flopping around like Clarabelle the Clown's over-sized shoes. Ever ingenious, I tried chewing an entire pack of Juicy Fruit in thirty seconds and doing one of those Heloise repair jobs, which never work when you most need them. (Where is Martha Stewart when you really need her? Probably at her broker's.)

"COME ON!" my impatient and unsympathetic spouse yelled at me, as I stood there, chipmunk cheeks crammed with gum, chewing furiously. "We've only got five minutes! You'll just have to carry them."

That is how I happened to attend a show at one of the world's most elegant hotels barefoot. I swept past the tuxedo-clad usher at the $80 million resort with the $35 million art collection, concealing my shoes beneath my wrap. The usher barely glanced at my very respectable long dress, but he did a double-take on the bare toes peeking out from under the hem, shook his head, and mumbled, under his breath, "Tourists!"

Summoning up whatever shred of dignity I could muster, I pulled myself up to my full five-foot three-inch height (OK….5' 2 and ¾") and followed the insolent usher to my seat in a ballroom crowded with bejeweled women in high heels.

Table ninety-one is a loooooooong walk when you're dodging the spiked heels of others while trying to appear nonchalant and carrying, rather than wearing, your shoes.

Major League Bugs

They sprayed for bugs in my junior high school classroom during Easter vacation. I know, because all the students were told to remove their books from their lockers prior to the spraying. I also know because the brown spray residue is still all over my classroom floor. It's right across the room from the spot where the roof leaks and forms a small lake when it rains.

When I say "bugs," I don't mean measly gnats. Oh, no! I'm talkin' major league cockroaches the size of a Buick, here, which we have euphemistically dubbed "water bugs." That is because they have been observed doing the backstroke in the lake.

I have a theory about these bugs. I think they are responsible for the books that keep disappearing. The cockroaches are carrying them off and stockpiling them. That may even be why the kids were told to remove their books from their lockers. No fools, these administrators, they wanted to keep the books out of the hands…..er, feelers….of the cockroaches.

Why would cockroaches want books? To keep them away from the termites that are eating the library bookshelves, of course. Yes, the crafty cockroaches know that if the termites corner the book food supply, the cockroaches have had it. And we're talking more than just food for thought here, folks!

So, the cockroaches have joined forces with the ants to stockpile their own source of book food. Ants, you say? Yes, ants. In the spring, I always have at least one fully developed anthill in my classroom. Two years ago it was directly behind my desk where I could point the little fellows out to my classes as object lessons in industry. Unfortunately, last year, the ants foolishly located near the lake in the back of the room. I think they were seeking to improve the property value of their hill. Break dancing students on their lunch hour killed the social-climbing ants that weren't flooded out.

The ants and the cockroaches have a Master Plan to outwit the library termites. Besides the locker books, which they have already infested and carried off, they are taking over the teachers' lounge. Ants in the sugar jar and pop bottles are a commonplace sight, but the cockroaches have really begun a full-scale assault. Last week, they captured Mr. Coffee Hill and a large, very dead cockroach was found, feet up, right in the middle of the community popcorn bowl.

What really brought all this home to me was when I absent-mindedly dropped a hunk of butter in the Pyrex measuring cup and popped it in to the microwave. Removing the cup, I discovered a sautéed cockroach, still sizzling in its own juices. Eeeeeuuuuwwww!

Employees in the upper echelons of the work world just don't know what they're missing in fringe benefits because they didn't go in to education!

My most horrible suspicion concerning the cockroaches, ants and missing textbooks is a truly frightening prospect. What if they're founding an alternative school? They may even be using their own version of the ABC's—Ants, Beatles and Cockroaches. They could be preaching insurrection right now and enlisting the aid of bookworms.

Spread the word.

When my friend Nelson, the history teacher, retired, it seems only apropos that his parting "gift" from his faculty friends was a very dead cockroach, feet up in an eraser box coffin. Retiring CEO's will never get that kind of mileage out of a gold watch.

Paper versus Plastic

Friends, grocers, countrymen, lend me your ears! I come to bury plastic bags, not to praise them.

How many of you have noticed the creeping epidemic of plastic bags instead of paper bags at your friendly neighborhood supermarket checkout counter? I hate these sleazy-looking slimy plastic bags. A plastic bag won't stand upright all by itself, like a good old brown paper bag will. A plastic bag, by its very nature, contributes to the trash problem by becoming trash immediately after you empty it.

Oh, sure, if you want to invest additional money in some sort of special hardware to make a bag re-usable, you can, but, by itself, in its virgin state, a plastic bag is a bust.

A paper bag, by contrast, has many uses. It can be used to line a garbage can and helps eliminate trash, not add to it. They can be used to wrap packages for mailing. They are a key ingredient in my Salvation Army sorting sprees as they stand bravely at attention, awaiting cast-off but still serviceable items. (A plastic bag would be lying down on the job.) Paper bags are useful for various crafts, including making kites and paper airplanes. Some famous writers like Emily Dickinson used to scribble their poems on paper bags and old envelopes. None other than Abe Lincoln himself is supposed to have written his Gettysburg Address on the back of an old envelope…(but enough of envelopes, back to bags).

Plastic bags have puny little handles, which you are supposed to use to hoist the sack and its contents. The way my grocery bags always are filled to overflowing, there's no way this could work.

You can make a mask out of a paper bag. Or, if your date is exceedingly ugly, you can put a bag over his or her head. As Rodney Dangerfield used to say, he often had blind dates who were two-baggers. A two-bagger, said Dangerfield, was when your date was so ugly that you put a bag over her head and then put a bag over your own head, so that nobody would know that you were going out with this person. Try Dangerfield's two-bagger technique with these new-fangled plastic bags and you'd really be in danger. You'd wind up one-half of a murder/suicide.

If God had meant grocers to use these plastic grocery store travesties, there would be some sort of sign. Having the handles rip off your plastic bag, as mine did recently, and watching one dozen eggs smash on the sidewalk as a result is not my idea of a favorable omen for the future success of these sleazy plastic grocery bags.

I have a good idea. Let's keep using the faithful old trusty brown paper bag. After all, as a much wiser person than I once ungrammatically said, "If it ain't broke, don't fix it!"

Mrs. Malaprop Lives

Some two hundred years ago an English author named Richard Brinsley Sheridan wrote a play entitled "The Rivals," in which a comic character called Mrs. Malaprop appeared.

Mrs. Malaprop tried to impress people by using big words. Unfortunately, she usually chose an incorrect word or expression that only sounded like the correct one.

Audiences laughed when Mrs. Malaprop ordered her niece to pursue a man "at the very pineapple of success" or told her to "illiterate" another man from her memory.

Modern-day malapropism is alive and well. Norm Crosby, the stand-up comic, has made a good living from this type of humor for years. I have painstakingly saved a few from my many years of junior high school teaching.

From a student paper: "Michael Jackson will be around for a very long time. I think he might even beat Elvis in population." (The student was half-right about Michael Jackson being around for a long time; his original nose, however, was not.)

"I stayed overnight with Bobby and we would go outside after his parents went to sleep and make a big bomb fire." (Must have been some fire!)

"I think if a nuclear war comes around, there will be survivors, but maybe after a month or two there will be kayos." (Yes. And there could be technical knock-outs, too!)

"When I am caught misbehaving, I get a good threshing." (I hope they use John Deere farm implements for this, although it sounds very painful.)

"My mom told me to turn my stereo down a few hundred disciples." (I often tell my daughter to turn her stereo down a few disciples, but it rarely does any good.)

"I told my little brother to quit playing records on my pornograph." (Ah, yes. The old pornograph.)

"The lady was in such poor condition that she needed artificial perspiration in the ambulance." (Right Guard, anyone?)

"Our coach yelled at us and said, 'You guys played like you were in a transom out there today!'" (Let's let that mental image sink in!)

"A good farmer must know how to irritate his crops." (It doesn't hurt if he knows how to irrigate them, either. I HATE when your crops get all testy after being irritated.)

From a Silvis School Board meeting of yesteryear and the lips of board member Bob C——: "I was in the hospital with a health problem so I've been pretty much incognito." Later, Bob said that he had "gone into conclusion." (He pretty much has, now, since he's dead.)I think it was the very same board meeting where Mr. R——

pronounced "parochial" as "paro-chee-al" while reading from an issue of "Ladies' Home Journal," that Bible of education. Oh, those wacky board members of the seventies! Oh, the hilarity!

"We've got to find out who's making these unanimous phone calls!"

(Yes. And it wouldn't hurt to find out who's making the anonymous ones, as well.)

"Stop trying to invade the issue!" (When they get to Poland, we'll unite to stop them.)

"I just told you one of the great antidotes of all time, and you act like you're in a comma." (Those pesky commas….the bane of all English students!)

ABC's World News tonight used closed captioning to report that Alan Greenspan, the Federal Reserve Chairman, was recovering from surgery "to remove an enlarged prostitute." As reported in the May 5th, 2003, issue of *Time* magazine, his wife, NBC correspondent Andrea Mitchell, responding to the blooper, said, "He should be so lucky!"

And, not to be out-done by faux pas on the national level, the local newspaper had a similar moment. In the April 30, 2003 issue of Davenport, Iowa's *Quad City Times* a report ran on a suicide bomber's attack in Tel Aviv, Israel. Three people were killed and forty-six injured in the attack at Mike's Place on the seafront walkway in Tel

Aviv, according to the article. As the history of such attacks was relayed, the article concluded by saying, "On June 1, 2001, a suicide bomber blew himself off in front of a disco at the southern end of the walkway, killing twenty-one people, most of them teenagers." A very sad story, but a humorous misprint, nonetheless.

In my junior high school teaching days, I used to be sent out to interview local radio and television personalities, asking them about their on-the-air bloopers. There were stories from reporters who reported the fall of the Berlin wall as "a wall of drips, bricking with mortar." There was one poor slob who referred to "Korean Var weterans."

And speaking of veterans (or weterans), veteran Channel Four (WHBF) sportscaster Don Sharp was doing play-by-play at one basketball game when, noticing that the player was consistently undershooting the basket, he announced, "His shorts are all shot." Quickly realizing his error, he recovered by adding, "Come to think of it, his shoes don't look so hot, either." Sharp also had the distinction of mispronouncing the word "putting" in saying, (while covering a golf tournament), "Here we have Mrs. _____ putting out on the 18th hole." Just one small change in pronouncing one vowel, and look what happens!

At basketball sectional tournament time in the state of Iowa, Tia Slater (then of KWQC, Channel 6, the NBC affiliate) says that a colleague turned to her at the news desk during the 10 o'clock news and said, "Well, Tia, it looks as though we have a lot of girls' sexual activity here in the state of Iowa tonight."

Fellow KWQC newsman Alan Byrne told a funny story that went like this: "I was announcing the change in a stadium playing surface from astro-turf to real grass and I said, 'The change from artificial grass to natural gas is right on schedule.'"

Bill Baker, who used to grace the air-waves as Bryan McGannon on what was then WQUA radio (1230 AM) once started his ad for a clothing store this way. "I snapped on the mike with real authority, " remembers Baker, "and announced: 'Attention! Fart small shoppers!'"

Shades of Mrs. Malaprop.

If You Cannot Find Osama: Bomb Iraq!

Just before we did the "shock and awe" number, dropping tons and tons of smart bombs on Iraq on April 9, 2003, I was sent this e-mail message by a friend of a friend. It had come from the desk of Frederick Antczak, Associate Dean for Academic Programs at the College of Liberal Arts and Sciences in Iowa City, Iowa (the University of Iowa, my alma mater), but Fred did not write it. A friend of his (whose name I do not know) actually wrote it, and it was forwarded to a friend of a friend and, well, you know how this works, don't you?

I found the ditty to be right on in its message (at least until May 1, 2011), which was as follows:

(Sung to the tune of "If You're Happy and You Know It")

If you cannot find Osama, bomb Iraq.

If the markets are a drama, bomb Iraq.

If the terrorists are frisky,

Pakistan is looking shifty,

North Korea's much too risky:

Bomb Iraq!

Although we have no allies with us: Bomb Iraq!

If we think someone has "dissed" us, Bomb Iraq!

So, to hell with the inspections,

Let's look tough for the elections,

Close your mind and take directions: Bomb Iraq!

It's "pre-emptive non-aggression": Bomb Iraq!

To prevent "mass destruction": Bomb Iraq!

They've got weapons we can't see

And that's good enough for me

'Cause it's all the proof I need: Bomb Iraq!

If you never were elected: Bomb Iraq!

If your mood is quite dejected: Bomb Iraq!

If you think Saddam's gone mad,

With the weapons that he had,

AND HE TRIED TO KILL YOUR DAD!

Bomb Iraq!

If your corporate fraud is growin': Bomb Iraq!

If your ties to it are showing: Bomb Iraq!

If your politics are sleazy,

And hiding it ain't easy,

And your manhood's getting queasy: Bomb Iraq!

Fall in line and follow orders: Bomb Iraq!

For our might knows not our borders: Bomb Iraq!

Disagree? We'll call it treason,

Let's make war, not love, this season,

Even if we have no reason: Bomb Iraq!

This contribution amused me mightily, and I took it with me to my volunteer reading on WVIK to the visually disabled, sharing it with the young clerk who was the night watchman of the volunteer shift. I had been reading to the blind and visually impaired, as a good deed, for over a year, and it had come to my attention that even the blind and visually impaired might be bored to near-death or coma by one entire hour filled with nothing but grocery prices and/or obituaries. So, during the three-minute break we were entitled to take at the half hour, I would normally bring in something "funny" from the newspaper. The Dave Barry article on "The Twelve Days of Christmas", for example, and why it was a horrible song...a sentiment with which I am in complete agreement.

Nobody had ever noticed or commented upon the fact that, during MY three minutes, I would (occasionally) digress and read something other than an obituary (the obituaries are "the favorite show." I'm wondering if the listeners are just making sure that they're not in them.)

The Big Rule in radio, of course, is "no dead air" and the other rule is that you not vary from the format. But the three minutes of air-time at the half hour was mine, all mine, and I determined that my not-yet-dead listeners— all three of them—who were, no doubt, huddled together in front of their special receivers in a tiny closet in Silvis or Colona or Milan somewhere, might enjoy hearing this little ditty. It was not a subversive act. I didn't even attempt to make it a secret act, telling John (the student watchman) of this humorous piece and singing a verse for him, before I entered the booth.

The night all hell broke loose was the first night that WVIK (Augustana College's public radio station) had installed its new equipment. Normally, nobody listens to anyone on the air at any time, I was then convinced, but, because they were having trouble regulating the volume levels of the new equipment, an engineer was (apparently) listening that night. I was only the second person to use the "new" equipment, which had been eagerly awaited for months, if not years.

Just as I launched into the second stanza of "If You Cannot Find Osama, Bomb Iraq" an engineer, who, henceforth, shall be dubbed "a pin-headed engineer" (actually, it was his shirt that was pin-striped, but who's keeping score, really?) burst in to my cubicle, frantically making the universally known "cut" gesture at the neckline and practically foaming at the mouth.

I carefully turned the button to place the channel on the network, which meant that pre-canned music would further anaesthetize the blind and almost-dead who were listening, picked up my things, and left. After all, I was an unpaid volunteer and the unpleasantness of this guy's frenzy was not to be over-estimated.

Mr. Pinhead then flew after me, following me into the parking lot, frothing with indignation, and quoting FCC (Federal Communications Commission) this, that and the other thing. It was snowing outside at the time. I said, "Calm down or you'll have a stroke." Then, I got in my car and drove away. When he followed me the second time, I think I said, "Chill and get a life," but I really don't remember. It was cold, he was sputtering something about agreeing with me "in principle" but upholding until death the FCC, and I was just cold.

At the bottom of the hill, I realized that I had left my sweater in the broadcast booth. I drove back up the hill to retrieve it. There were now *five* "engineers" all huddled together outside the door of the studio. They were all a-flutter-twit! As I entered I said, "Gee! This must be the most excitement you guys have had in years!" My favorite engineer, Gary, quickly ducked his head and scurried down the hall, but Mr. Pinhead, again, pursued me into the parking lot, practically apoplectic. It was all "FCC this" and "FCC that." Interestingly enough, although I made several subsequent phone calls to various mucky mucks, trying to find out exactly WHAT the FCC "rules and regulations" might have been, they could never be located, and I probably would have to correspond with Colin Powell's son personally (then the head of the FCC) to find out what horrible fate awaited someone like me who dared to sing a satirical ditty on the air that was not politically correct at this moment in history, when we are all about marching into countries that were leaving us alone and taking them over.

About this time, various anti-war demonstrations were taking place. I chose to join the one at the Writers' Studio, which I knew would be full of people who might be very full of themselves, many of them pontificating on the subject of war in "original" verse. The original verse was pretty bad, in general. Only Lawrence Ferlinghetti's poem held my attention, but, when I got out my accordion and invited the crowd to join me in a sing-along, let's just say that it got the crowd's attention!

I had inherited the accordion from my cousin, Lois's husband, Larry, on the Fourth of July, when we traveled to St. Louis to visit him for the last time, as he was terminally ill with liver cancer. Larry and I had for years shared a secret hatred of the accordion, which both of us were forced to learn to play against our will. We smuggled his old accordion down from the attic and into the trunk of our car while my husband was in the bathroom, and I had been having a great deal of fun getting it out and thinking up devilish ways to use it. This was one.

I also remember that each and every other participant in that night's event spent at least ten minutes introducing themselves, going on about how they taught here or there. (One guy said he had written six plays. I said, to the person seated next to me, "I don't think that Neil Simon has anything to worry about.") As I write this, there is no college or university, locally, that I have not been affiliated with, in one capacity or another. I, however, chose to remain anonymous.

So it was that, in the next morning's paper, as it wrote up the event, it said, "An anonymous woman with an accordion took the podium." The newspaper went on to recite the first couple of stanzas of "If You Cannot Find Osama: Bomb Iraq!"

When I came home late from "tacos", my husband wanted to know where I had been.

I said, "I was playing my accordion at an anti-war rally."

He said, "Sure you were," rather wryly.

I also made a stand-up appearance at our local comedy club on the final Wednesday of February. I worked this in during the Wednesday night "taco night" with the girls, so that my husband was none the wiser. Our marriage is a little like that of Arnold Schwarzenegger and Maria Shriver (now on the rocks as of May 10, 2011), so I try to keep a low political profile, when possible. I included a lot of political humor in my secret Penguin's Comedy Club routine, along the lines of, "What did Gennifer Flowers say, when asked if her affair with Bill Clinton was similar to that of Bill and Monica Lewinsky?"

A: "Close, but no cigar."

I also shared the joke that historians had decided to call Clinton's eight years in office "Sex Between the Bushes." But nevermind about that.

On that last Wednesday in February at Penguin's Comedy Club, it was my singing of "If You Cannot Find Osama, Bomb Iraq!" that was the featured set-piece of the evening's festivities. My tale of how Mr. Pin-headed (ok, pin-striped) Engineer Person pursued me into the parking lot of WVIK (next time: mace, I said) was greeted with chuckles. I also told about the after-math of my faux pas on the air at WVIK, the NPR affiliate.

The morning after I "dared to be different" on the air, I got a phone call from the woman who was the volunteer coordinator. Unfortunately, the woman chose to call me at 8:00 a.m. It is well-known by my friends that calls before 10:00 a.m. are ill-advised. She went into a long, droning speech about how we couldn't have this sort of shenanigans on the air.

I was half asleep and so tired that, at one point, I laid the telephone down on the pillow next to me until the droning stopped. Then, I picked up the phone and shared the information with the nice lady that if Mr. Pin-headed Engineer Person pursued me in to the parking lot while yapping at my heels one more time, I would be forced to use mace. I cheerily asked her to pass this information along to Mr. Pin-headed Engineer Person.

I also spent futile hours making phone calls to various mucky mucks affiliated with the station, in an attempt to find out exactly what the FCC "rules and regulations" actually were. I remember asking, "Was it my singing? Was that what set them off?"

I never found out what the FCC rules and regulations were. After the early-morning phone call from the previously nice volunteer lady (who is now decidedly frosty), I got a letter from her, warning me that political commentary of this sort had no place in a democracy, since my opinion did not support our fearless leader's (George W.'s) bombing of a nearly defenseless country that hadn't attacked us.

After we actually bombed these poor schmucks back to the StoneAge, in keeping with George W. Bush's "Whack-A-Mole" foreign policy commitment (that is what the experts actually call it), I gave up any thought that the lives of innocent civilians and servicemen could be saved by the likes of me, and quit singing "If You Cannot Find Osama, Bomb Iraq!" but I still think it's a keen song, and I want to give public credit to Frederick's friend, whoever he is, and say, "Hey! The blind and visually-impaired listeners with a special receiver within a 10 mile radius of WVIK in Rock Island, Illinois, are behind you!" And, since we did get Osama bin Laden on May 1, 2011, now we're only bombing Iraq, Afghanistan and Libya.

I also wrote a letter back to Diane (the previously nice volunteer lady) saying that I didn't really think that the walls of WVIK would come tumbling down because I sang two stanzas of "the forbidden song," as I now call this ditty, which goes right alongside the "forbidden dance," the Lambada, in infamy and history's judgment.

And, if all else fails, and you cannot find Osama: Bomb Iraq! Nothing of value left there, anyway, at this point.

Hooters Hilarity

I am not sure when Hooters became a factor in my life. Was it when one of my son's girlfriends, in an unsuccessful bid to make him jealous and stampede him towards matrimony, took a second job there? She was commuting to Hooterville from her day job with an insurance agency at the time and getting only four hours of sleep, so the job did not last long, but it caused several humorous comments around our house, although my son was not that amused, and the relationship soon faltered for other reasons. But Hooters had jiggled its way into my consciousness, even though I had never been inside a Hooters restaurant.

I saw the inside of a Hooters restaurant for the first time on September 11, 2001. I was at a Sylvan Learning Center conference in Baltimore, Maryland, in what is known as the Inner Harbor, residing on the thirty-eighth floor of Baltimore's tallest hotel, directly across the street from Baltimore's version of New York City's World Trade Center. Terrorists had just hit the twin towers of New York City with commercial airliners. I was mesmerized by the sight, "live," on my morning television screen. I realized that life as we knew it would never be the same again.

I had just come out of the bathroom clad in only a towel. I sank to the bed, still wearing only the towel. I didn't leave my room for hours, watching both assaults on the Twin Towers in real time until I was called by my employee, Chris, from the hotel lobby.

"Aren't you coming down?" she asked.

It was now about noon. All the carnage had taken place early in the morning of that fateful day.

I explained that there wasn't a workshop or a Sylvan speaker of any kind who could hold my attention when history was being made on television and our world was seemingly spinning out of control. First, there were the two planes hitting the Trade Center. Then, there were reports of a plane hitting the Pentagon and another going down in Pennsylvania. No one knew what to expect or how big this conspiracy might be.

Chris, my faithful employee on the phone, repeated, "Aren't you coming down?"

I explained that I was still glued to my TV set and I wondered how it was that anyone would leave theirs at this critical moment in our nation's history.

She said, "Well, maybe that's because they evacuated every floor above the fourth floor hours ago. The authorities aren't sure whether there are any other Eastern seaport cities that have been targeted by the terrorists, and they are taking the precaution because this is the tallest building in Baltimore, directly across the street from *their* World Trade Center."

Oh. Well. Nobody had 'splained it to me like THAT before!

So, I quickly gathered up what worldly belongings I thought I might need if I were barred from returning to my room for a long period of time, realizing, as I stuffed a book and writing material and comfortable walking shoes in to my tote bag, that I was hungry.

This is where Hooters comes in, again. The city of Baltimore had come to an almost complete halt, like a flower shutting its petals for the night. The Inner Harbor shops at the trendy mall were all closed or closing. There was yellow crime scene tape around their WTC building, and armed men with rifles were guarding it. We couldn't even walk on that side of the street as we approached the Inner Harbor mall.

Where were we going to eat? It was now afternoon, and we were hungry. The policeman we asked directed us to Hooters, which had the distinction of being almost the only restaurant in Inner Harbor Baltimore operating on 9/11/01. So, hi-ho, hi-ho, it's off to Hooters we would go.

How surreal is it to be watching the airplane attack on the World Trade Center replaying, over and over on national television, while a jiggly blonde in tight, short shorts asks you for your order in Hooters-speak?

"What's wrong with this picture?" I asked Chris, my second-in-command, "President George W. Bush is exhorting the nation to remain calm, and I am ordering chicken wings from someone in microscopically tight shorts with Bambi on her name tag."

In the fall semester of 2003, while teaching at one of the six local colleges in the area, Hooters once again became relevant. This was a class designed to prepare students to write resumes and go through interviews in the real world. I had gone to considerable time and effort to arrange for real interviewers from industry to come to my classroom to make the experience more realistic. One gentleman, in fact, worked part-time as an interviewer for Sedona, a part-time placement agency. Another gentleman had hired and fired at Deere & Company before retirement and yet another had done the same for Alcoa.

Prior to the actual interview date, one student, whom I shall refer to as Courtney because of her resemblance to "Friends" star Courtney Cox, asked me if she could interview for a position as a waitress at Hooters during her mock interview.

Initially, I was tempted to say no, which would have been a knee-jerk reaction to the name of the restaurant itself. Then, I thought about this girl's major: American Sign Language. When I had asked her what her career goals were with a degree in ASL, she had said, "To get up on outta' here." She said that she assumed that she would have to move to a large city to find work as an ASL interpreter, and I concurred, saying that her other choice would be to complete her ASL degree and also obtain a teaching credential. When I asked her if she wanted to do this, and, therefore, wanted her interview to be with a potential school district employer, she had responded, "What do you think I am…crazy?"

She went on to say that children were not her goal in life…ever. It seemed that the prospect of working with them, full-time, had all the appeal of a root canal for Courtney.

Therefore, when Courtney asked me if she could interview for a position as a waitress at Hooters, knowing that her current jobs were as a waitress for Applebee's and as a weekend cocktail waitress on one of our Mississippi River gambling boats, I thought, "Who am I to interfere with her life's calling?" It appeared that waitressing was her immediate and future goal. Possibly her past, her present and her future.

Therefore, I said that she could, indeed, interview to become a member of the Hooters wait staff.

She immediately countered with, "Can I wear something low-cut and plunging for the interview?"

"Well, Courtney, that doesn't seem like a good idea. You should dress as our text-book advises. Wear something that you would wear to church."

Who knew that Courtney was a member of the Church of What's Happening Now!?

Since I knew that, hearing the very word Hooters would cause a raised eyebrow or two, I made my husband call the male interviewer, whom I shall call Larry, the night before, to warn him, in advance, that the ASL girl was going to be interviewing for a position as a wait person at that establishment.

Apparently, Larry (the interviewer) thought my husband was kidding.

I should mention here that Larry is not the kind of guy to get rattled easily. He has a loose personality, spent eight years in the Navy, and likes to tell a risqué joke as much as the next guy. I commented that he was the only one of our friends who did not wear underwear.

The person with whom I shared this fact said, "How do you know?"

I know because his wife told me, of course. I am taking it on faith, just as I hope that he has taken it on faith that I did NOT intentionally set him up for what was to occur on the fateful day of the mock interview. I had no idea that Courtney would behave as though there were no filter between her brain and her mouth.

The interview started with one of the ten questions I had distributed to the class in advance, to help them prepare, which was, "What do you consider your greatest asset?" These questions had been culled from the most-commonly asked questions in real job interviews. It should have been "safe."

The Hooters girl immediately answered enthusiastically, "I've got great boobs!" and came close to flashing us all.

The interview was turning into the most surreal teaching day of a thirty-three year career. And I've had some pretty surreal teaching days!

This response caused Larry to redden noticeably. He shared later that now he didn't know exactly where to direct his gaze. Memories of his former days at Alcoa, complete with classes on sexual harassment and grounds for same were rushing to the forefront of his heated brain. He realized that he was treading on dangerous ground, if this were a real-world environment.

I had told my class that they were to score the interviews. Fortunately, this particular batch was not being filmed, although earlier ones had been. The class was sitting in the audience, and was told to pretend that there was an invisible Gardol shield separating them from the interviewer and the interviewee. However, the snickering had begun. Even though they were not to let on by remark or interaction that they were present, as, indeed, they were not supposed to BE present, it was difficult for us all. There were categories for the class to score constituting "attire," "ability to sell one's self," "knowledge of the company" and "follow-up questions," among others.

The next question Larry asked was, "What do you consider your greatest weakness?"

"Probably my ass," said Courtney. Although she then lapsed in to a discussion of her abdominal muscles and other body parts that left us all gasping in a futile attempt to remain quiet, as instructed.

In the back of the room, I was finding this difficult myself and called out, "Larry: you're old enough to remember *Lost in Space* . Picture an alarm noise (Ka-Yu-Gah! Ka-You-Gah!) and a voice saying, "Danger, Will Robinson! Danger!"

Larry bravely continued, attempting to regain his equilibrium, although a tell-tale blush had crept up his usually pale white Swedish cheeks and neck. After determining that Courtney currently worked on a gambling boat on weekends as a cocktail waitress, he asked her, "Have you ever had anyone you were waiting on do or say something inappropriate when you were waiting on them? And how did you handle it?"

Courtney responded, in a very puzzled voice, "Like what?"

This put the onus of naming names and describing offenses clearly on Larry, who had already decided that he was skating on very thin ice.

He moved on, asking, "How did you get along with your supervisor on the Pair of Dice?" (fictitious name)

Courtney said, "Well, once, when I left to go to the rest room, he said to me, when I returned, in front of everybody, 'Either you sneaked outside to have a cigarette or you took one gigantic dump.'"

This disclosure seemed to leave the entire class gasping for air. I know it wasn't doing too much for me, as I tried to figure out if any self-respecting executive in the entire state of Illinois would ever volunteer to "mock interview" members of my class again.

At this exact point, Courtney looked out at the assembled class members (through the Gardol shield) and said, "This interview isn't going too well, is it?"

Talk about your understatements.

Larry finally concluded the interview. I don't remember how, and I doubt if he does, either. We collapsed in the hall outside the classroom in helpless mirth and Larry said, "I think I need a shot of Jack Daniels."

Later, I read that Hooters has launched an airline and visions of Courtney flashing the passengers as they deplaned entered my head. I also saw the following item, which I shall report verbatim:

Dateline: Belleville, Illinois – Parents complained that Superintendent Darrel Hardt took junior high students to a Hooters restaurant during a school trip. Hardt said the chain restaurant was the only inexpensive place that would accommodate twenty-six students.

I think I know this Superintendent. Wasn't he once a coach?

True Tales of Child-Raising

(*These anecdotes were typed up and mailed as 1990's Christmas letter.)

Anecdote #1:

Stacey is very musical and loves to sing. They told us at pre-school that she "loves to sing loud." Not well, but loud. Ever since she was a tiny little girl, I have always sung "I Feel Pretty" from "West Side Story" to her as we toweled her off after her bath.

Imagine my surprise, when, on the line, "Who's that pretty girl in the mirror there? (What mirror, where?) Who can that attractive girl be?" I finally heard what she had been singing all this time.

"Who's that pretty girl in the mirror there? Who can that tractor girl be?"

With a Dad who put in 36 years with John Deere, it seems like, if those weren't the *real* lyrics, for her, they should be.

Anecdote #2:

While driving across the "Mighty Mickey-ssippi," which is what three-year-old Stacey used to call the Mississippi river, I heard her singing along to that old tune "Hang on, Sloopy." She was singing, "Hang on, Snoopy!"

When I corrected her, she changed it to, "Hang on, Stupid!"

Anecdote #3:

We enjoyed the phone call home from Stacey and Steve and Regina, who had gone to Chicago ("Cago" to Stacey). "Are you in Chicago?" Craig asked.

"No," she said, somewhat puzzled, "I'm in a hotel room."

Anecdote #4:

I was amused to see how puzzling our familiar idioms can be to foreigners.

I clearly remember my Swedish college student, Per Olof Gustaffsson, writing me from Duse Udde on Lake Vanerne in Sweden that it was "snowing cats and dogs."

I asked Stacey, innocently enough, "How do you like them apples?" one day, and she responded, quite seriously, "What apples, Mom?"

Anecdote #5:

When Scott, then age 3, observed a dead raccoon on the way home from his grandparents' house, he said, "That raccopoon was kicking my dad's car!" For some unknown reason, he then began calling the dead "raccopoon" Sparky.

Anecdote #6:

We were working hard to toilet-train son Scott and to get him to use "the potty," as he knew he should, rather than simply relieving himself in the great outdoors. But, you know how it is when, as his sister Stacey used to put it, "I'm pwetty busy pwaying."

One day during this time, he came in the house with a particularly guilty look on his face. Finally, unable to control himself and craving absolution, he burst out, "Nobody went potty over there by the swing set!"

Anecdote #7:

First sexual question, asked by Scott when age 3: "Mommy, does you got a tail?"

Anecdote #8:

Stacey has an active imagination. The other day she told me a very detailed story involving going to the moon.

She got to the moon on a rocket; it was cold there. So far, so good. When she arrived, she found Linda, Nelson and "Beff" were there, along with their dog, eating pickles and French fries.

I asked, "Was Neil Armstrong there?"

"No, Mom," she said, very exasperated with my denseness, *"Nelson!"*

Springtime Memories

I am reminded of the time that I attempted to do something nice for my Dad. It was spring, and I thought that he would be thrilled if I were to wash the car, unbidden.

He probably would have liked it, if I had not driven the car onto the very wet back yard lawn. As I hosed it off, the car proceeded to sink into the lawn up to its hubcaps, although this escaped my attention at the time.

When I tried to drive it from the crime scene, things took a turn for the worse. I could not get the car out of the lawn.

I heard someone whistling as they walked by on the sidewalk below. It was Chet Schmitz, (an awesome whistler, who later played professionally in a Symphony orchestra), walking home. I summoned Chet and asked his advice, but he was convulsed with laughter, which didn't help at all.

Eventually, my father had to jack the car OUT of the lawn on 2x4's.

I was using an old Rex-Air to clean the interior of the car, a vacuum cleaner that had a bottom level into which you put water, vacuuming the inside of the car and pulling the thing too far over. Water spilled over onto the electrical switch. I was being electrocuted.

I couldn't let go of the vacuum, so I began yelling, as loudly as I could, hoping that my father would come help me. He was inside the kitchen, watching at the time.

Finally, I was able to pull my numb and tingling hand from the vacuum cleaner and went in the house, badly shaken.

"Didn't you hear me yelling?" I asked.

"Well, yes," he answered mildly, "but I just thought you were yelling at some friends."

I was once put in charge of another electrical appliance…in this case, an electric lawn-mower. My father thought it was a wonderful alternative to a gas mower, as you never had to start it. You merely had to plug it in and start it up.

You did, however, have to be careful that you didn't cut the cord, and, on hills, I was told, always vacuum DOWN, not UP.

I forgot this and the vacuum ran over my tennis shoe. All I could see was that my white Keds were turning red from blood. The mower had rolled over my foot. (DOWN, standing above it, not UP!)

I limped into the house, where my sister and I removed what was left of my shoe, to discover that my toe was intact. Only my toe-nail was missing. Grim as that sounds, I have seldom felt luckier!

When I was in sixth grade, a bunch of us went to camp. I don't remember much about camp, other than that the cabins were bug-infested, dark and unpleasant. We had only bunk beds and communal showers and bathroom(s) and we had to walk a long way to get to them.

There was a dance at some point during "camp." I was wearing a chemise dress, then the style. Someone said it looked like a maternity dress; I was mortified and had a horrible time at the dance.

A tree had fallen on the trampoline.

Friend Beverley and I attempted to take a canoe out, but we couldn't agree on a direction and so the canoe overturned while we argued about whether to go this direction or that.

On the last day of camp, everyone was picked up by the Siessegers. I don't know why they left me there. I suspect that Jane didn't like me and just wanted to abandon me in this hell-hole.

I sat there on the edge of that crumpled, broken metal trampoline for hours, wondering how I was going to get home from Camp Wapsie-Y or whatever-the-hell it was called. It should have been called Camp Hellacious. It had been a truly horrible week in every respect, and now I was marooned there for life!

Finally, after it became clear that no one was ever coming to pick me up (all the other car-poolers having left with the Siessegers), I found a phone and called home. No one was there except for my sister, who was too young to drive.

I ended up having to ride home with the camp counselor. To this day, the word "camp" does not summon good memories.

Golf

I once had a fellow working at a golf course tell me that I "ought to write a book" about my experiences. I don't know if writing an entire book is merited, but I do think that my experiences while golfing are worth mentioning.

My first introduction to golf came when my mother decided, when I was in the sixth grade, that she was going to hire the coach of our local golf team to teach Candy Hatfield and me to golf. It was summertime, and Coach Duvall, who had had a state championship golf team in the state the preceding year, was willing, if not eager, to take on the instruction of two twelve-year old girls who had never played the game.

I should mention, first, that my mother's clubs were genuine antiques. They were all old and tweedy-looking, with little spirals of wire sticking out from where they were wrapped around the heads of these things. I was totally embarrassed to have to play with anything that looked this bad. And the bag was worse.

To counteract the image created by the really crappy golf clubs, I wore my new blue suede shoes. These were definitely cool. The song had just come out (OK, so I'm dating myself; what do I care?) and I had these really nifty blue slip-on shoes. They were comfortable, too, which was good, since Candy and I didn't have a ride to the country club and were going to have to walk there over a long, winding, gravel road.

I always got the feeling that Mr. Duvall was not really all that enthused about playing golf with a couple of twelve-year old girls who happened to be teachers' kids. Why would I get that impression? Oh, I don't know. Maybe because all we ever did was chip and putt. No REAL playing, just chipping and putting on the hole closest to the winding gravel road. This particular hole placement will soon become important in my story.

It was while chipping and putting and putting and chipping…especially the chipping….that, not knowing my own strength, I hit one that soared out onto the road and knocked the back window out of a passing pick-up truck. There was a screech of tires and the bewildered driver made a bee-line for us and our coach.

Mr. Duvall never ever let me forget about the broken-window-in-the-truck incident. Of course, my family had to pay for the broken window, and of course it became a giant family joke.

However, the worst of those ill-fated lessons at age twelve was yet to come. When Candy and I completed our day's lesson and returned to the clubhouse, hot and tired in the July heat, I took off my new blue suede shoes, put them in my golf bag, and went inside. We got a pop (Orange Nehi, if I remember correctly) and, when we returned to the spot on the sidewalk outside the clubhouse where my golf bag still sat forlornly in its pull cart, my shoes were gone. To this day, I don't know who took them or why, but I DO know that walking home some 5 miles, barefoot, over a gravel road does nothing to instill a love of the game of golf in the neophyte player.

After my marriage, I returned to this course as a young bride. It was the Fourth of July weekend, and hotter than the proverbial pistol. I had not played golf since the ill-fated lessons with Candy, but my husband, an accomplished golfer, thought it would be a good idea for us to take up the game as a couple. I was less sure, but willing to give it a go at the club to which my parents belonged.

The game was really going poorly. I still think that golf should be a 7-hole sport. Seven holes is about right. Nine holes is too long and eighteen holes is like the Bataan Death March. I have never been able to hit a golf ball with a three of anything, and, at this point in my golfing career, no one had seen fit to inform me of the existence of the five-wood or other more useful clubs. I was still in the mode where I might as well have been issued a large bat, which I could use to just pound golf balls into the surface of the course. God knows I couldn't hit anything up in the air with a three (wood or iron, makes no difference) and yet I had been told that this was the club of choice for the fareway. So I soldiered manfully (or womanfully) along, driving golf ball after golf ball about 3 feet, and hitting it yet again.

After seven holes of this foolishness in blazing heat, I was ready to quit. And, apparently, so was my husband, if you can believe that.

(And I know that you can.) Is there anything worse than being a good golfer saddled with someone who has to hit it seven times to go 100 yards?

Anyway, I talked him into quitting after the seventh hole, which ended up back near the row of cabins leading into the golf club. It wasn't really that hard. It was hot. I was horrible. And so, after seven holes, we headed toward the gravel road entrance that went right past the cabins where some lived during the summer.

It was then that we became aware of a crowd that had gathered in front of the third cabin on the left-hand side of the gravel road leading to the clubhouse. An ambulance was parked in front of the cabin and a very exhausted nurse was shouting, "Does anyone here know CPR?"

As luck would have it, my husband and I had just completed a CPR course at Illini Hospital in Silvis, Illinois, where we had all pumped the chest of Resusci-Annie and learned about establishing airways and compressions and all the rest of it. In fact, I was carrying the "reminder" in my purse that very minute, and I immediately got it out. The exhausted woman, who turned out to be a nurse who had been administering CPR to Frank Barger, saw this and, always willing to help, I said, "We know CPR."

Thus began Mr. Toad's Wild Ride in the Independence ambulance. Why they sent the ambulance out with just a driver is a very good question, which I will have to ask someone some day. Mr. Barger, who was the usher and ticket-taker at the town movie theater, had been wallpapering at the nearby cabin when he was felled by a heart attack. The nurse next door established an airway (he was already bagged) and began CPR, but, as anyone who has ever done CPR knows firsthand, it is an exhausting procedure and one person, alone, is soon worn out.

"Get in the ambulance!" this stranger cried.

And so it began.

One compression, followed by a curve in the road. One of us would fly into the side of the ambulance while the other attempted to compress Mr. Barger's chest, as we had learned to do in class. I felt like a piece of popcorn inside a popcorn popper.

Mr. Barger did not look good. Much as I would have liked to help Trudy's dad, he was blue when we started working on him. I doubt if he ever had a fighting chance.

When we reached the ambulance garage, the attendants rushed to his aid and he was wheeled into the ambulance on a gurney. No one thought to turn off the ambulance siren, which blared loudly and ricocheted off the walls of the ambulance garage. Finally, practically deafened by the noise, I climbed over the partition dividing the back from the driver's seat area and began fiddling with dials until I located the right one.

Then, I followed the gurney into the hospital and tried to find out if Mr. Barger was okay. He had once kicked me out of "Jack the Ripper" for sneaking in the back door from the alley without paying, but I bore him no ill will.

Alas, although a sinus rhythm was established, Mr. Barger could not be saved. And thus my love of the game of golf grew by leaps and bounds.

On our next outing, an event sponsored by a local tavern whose owner we knew, a small ground squirrel was found, dead, near my ball. It appeared that I might have hit and killed him, although, to this day, I maintain that the beer truck which patrolled the course had run over him. The cow that I hit, right between the eyes, in a field across the fence from the Independence course, fared much better, living testament to my poor aim.

I went into golf retirement for many years. Some would say not as many as necessary, but those are the nay-sayers among us. I did not play golf again for many years.

It was not until May of 1996 that my husband and I joined Short Hills Country Club in East Moline, Illinois. I wanted to join for the social aspects, but my husband really likes to play golf, which must be because he can play golf. I, on the other hand, was still beating balls in to the ground with various golf implements. I never met a divot I didn't like.

I was enticed in to joining by a friend (one wonders now), who invited us to partner with them in the All-You-Can-Eat Shrimp Boil. In return for pretending to be a golfer during a two-ball event that featured six-member teams playing best ball, I would be rewarded with all the shrimp I could eat. It was too good an offer to pass up.

My husband and I said, "Sign us up!"

The night of the event it was pouring down rain. There were three carts. My partner and I (I was riding with Bert) had the only one without a roof, so, of course, we got soaked throughout our playing time, while the other two couples remained relatively dry.

There were several incidents that did not bode well for our team. For one thing, as our cart drove up the very first incline, my clubs fell off and the cart behind us ran over them. Apparently they had not been properly secured by the caddies.

Second, Bert thought that a couple on the first hole we reached was "just practicing" and went out on to the green, threw down his ball, and began taking practice putts. I was in awe. I thought that these people were, indeed, playing in the All You Can Eat Shrimp Boil Two-ball, and, as it turns out, I was right. Bert had just committed a heinous faux pas.

Third, our team, never really much into reading the rules, was teeing off pretty randomly when a guy in another cart came racing over to inform us that it was "women on odd," "men on even.". As he approached us at warp speed, he could not brake quickly enough. In addition to running over Bert's wife's foot, he tore up about 30 feet of the fareway when his cart brakes locked. Later, my brother-in-law became very concerned, as this was "his" hole to police, and it now had a huge skid mark that needed re-sodding.

We limped back to the clubhouse in the rain, where I stood in line a long time for my turn to use the one hairdryer. I looked like a drowned rat. Finally, it was my turn and I dried my golden locks. When I looked halfway normal, I went upstairs to claim the all-you-can-eat shrimp, only to learn that (a) everyone on my team of six except me had already finished eating (b) they were now in the bar (c) all the shrimp were gone.

In order to further improve my very rusty golf game, I also joined the EWG (Executive Women's Golf League) about this same time. This league met at a very long and very narrow course that I have been told is one of the most difficult courses in this area to play. Who knew? All I know is that I never broke 70 (for 9 holes) at this course, hold the record for getting caught in the automatic sprinkler, and frequently had to shoot into a crowd of deer.

Glynn's Creek, the course in question, has long had a problem with deer who have become so tame that they will come right up to you, during your shot, and eat the bark off a nearby tree. It's as though they want to taunt you by saying, "Hey, loser! Look at me! I can eat the bark off this tree and you can't do anything about it!"

At various times the authorities relax the rules on shooting deer out of season and various card-carrying members of the NRA enthusiastically troop out to the golf course to "thin the herd." This process becomes more urgent since tics carry Lyme disease, and we all know that tics live on deer. (Don't we?) I once shot into a family of four Bambi-types, a Momma, a Daddy, and two baby deer. They were nonchalant. They seemed to know that my shot could do them no real harm.

I was always getting caught in the sprinkler system at Glynn's Creek because we teed off at 5:00 p.m. By the time Jane (my partner) and I made it to the ninth hole, it was getting dark. This was because we were so bad that we had to take about 20 strokes per hole, between us. The sprinkler system would kick in, automatically, because it was dusk. Jane was even worse than me, which I did not think was possible. I don't think she will be mad at me for saying this. If she is, then I take it back.

My handicap at this time was 36, the very highest handicap possible for nine holes. I had nowhere to go but up. Or, actually, down, in terms of handicap strokes.

My friend Judy, who had had one lesson from a very good pro at Glynn's Creek named Kurt Schnell, recommended that I take a lesson from him. She said that he was expensive, but well worth the money. I certainly couldn't get any worse, as I was basically just pounding golf balls into the fareway with my three-wood, harming small animals, and getting soaked while playing.

I signed up for a lesson with Mr. Schnell. I think Kurt is now a pro in Omaha, Nebraska. He was a very good teacher who used both verbal instruction, pictures, and a video-camera, to actually film me in action. Mr. Schnell gave me one lesson, laughed a great deal, and, soon thereafter, moved to Omaha. If quizzed, he would be able to testify that I have the worst form of any female golfer he has ever seen. I do everything wrong. I bend my arm when I hit the ball. I was slicing it to the right in a lovely arcing motion that was doing nothing to lower my 36 handicap. There is no proof to the rumor, however, that he moved to Omaha *after* he saw me play.

The first thing Mr. Schnell mentioned was, "You're holding the club all wrong."

He instructed me in the basic "Hello, Mr. Club" hand-shaking grip, which I still use today. If I have not said, "Hello, Mr. Club," I have not addressed the ball, and it will, for sure, go soaring directly into the nearest right-hand sand trap or tree. Always right. Never left. Since I am playing with a Herky the Hawk ball currently, I have modified this to "Hello, Mr. Herky." As soon as I shoot Herky into a lake on the right, I will go back to "Hello, Mr. Club."

Mr. Schnell was able to lower my handicap from 36 to 23, with one lesson, a video-camera and plenty of laughter. I remember being asked to do everything with a 7-iron.This was fine by me. I did not aspire to be better than a 23-handicap for 9 holes, but I still was frustrated by my lack of consistency. It was typical for me to hit 9-6-9-5-9-4 and so on. I could even par a hole or two, on occasion. But the next hole would be an 8 or a 9.

My long game improved, but my short game did not. This may be because I was using the Purple Putter of Death, on the grounds that it matched my clubs, which were Blue Light Specials from K-Mart. These clubs are about the weight of a tire iron, at least twenty years old, and totally ineffectual.

I invested in some new clubs, some new irons and a new putter, an Omega, as recommended by the EWG women's golf clinic staff. This did nothing to improve my putting, but I felt better about myself. At least I was stylish! I also liked the name: Omega.

The first club purchase, however, that literally changed my life and my game forever was a five-wood that I purchased at Sam's Wholesale Club. I bought it the night before the Ladies Invitational Member/Guest event. Everyone had told me what a great event this was. You could invite a guest to play for a pittance (golf, otherwise, being a pricey proposition). There was a lunch. Nobody mentioned that the event was EIGHTEEN HOLES LONG and that almost everyone who participated was a real golfer who was at least seventy years of age. I think it was a rule that you had to have blue hair.

I do not like doing anything before 10:00 a.m., and the tee-off time was 9:00 a.m. I set my alarm clock, so that I would be up when my friend Judy picked me up, but I set it (accidentally) for 9:00 p.m., not 9:00 a.m.

Therefore, when Judy arrived at my door, all cheery and ready to go, I was still in my pajamas. I was neither cheery nor ready. I had my brand-new still shrink-wrapped club ready, however, in a nano-second, and we were off, attempting to make it to the club before the tee-off time.

We did not quite make the tee-off time. We were late. We had to find "Number Three Hole" to join the group (our foursome) that had just left without us. I had no idea where the Number Three Hole was. I had always just ridden along in the cart, enjoying the great outdoors and the woodland creatures, warning them, you might say. We probably looked like a female version of Dumb and Dumber as we randomly tried out various holes to see if they were "three."

We did find Number Three, however, and, indeed, our fellow two-some had already driven and were mid-fairway. They were gracious enough to allow us to tee up and join them, however, and I stepped up, removed the shrink wrap from my new Big Bertha, said, "Hello, Mr. Club" (I was not yet using Herky). Not having anywhere to discard the shrink wrap I had just removed from my club, I slapped it firmly on my butt. My partner almost cardiac arrested.

Judy said, "You mean you have never played with that club before now?"

"Of course not. If I had, would it still have the shrink wrap on it?"

Well, friends and neighbors, I want to let you know that a five-wood is the name of the game if you are a female golfer who cannot hit a three-wood to save her life. (Or anyone else's, judging from our unfortunate experience with Mr. Barger).

Now, I began the usual "hack and run" motif, where I hit it at least six or seven times to get to the edge of the green. At this point, one of the blue-haired golfers drove her cart up to us, all in a lather, and said, "If you hit it more than seven times, pick it up!"

I responded, "Lady, if I pick it up after only seven strokes I won't ever get to finish a hole."

She then hissed, "Read the rules! Read the rules!"

Finding this amusing and in a cavalier and fey mood, I said, "Rules? Rules? We don't need no steenking rules."

This did not seem to amuse Ms. Blue Hair.

We continued our play.

Suddenly, the first nine, which had taken a very long time, indeed, to complete, was over. Quelle horror! This ordeal was supposed to last for ANOTHER nine holes. I said, "Judy, looks like we will be eating lunch somewhere else," turned the cart around, and we left.

To this day, I have not played in another Member/Guest function.

I'm still out there, however, so small animals: beware!

Sam I Am

When I was in college, I gave my parents a Siamese cat, which they named Sam. Sam was an ornery critter. I remember my journey to pick him out. I thought it was cute that he hid under a chair, only occasionally reaching out to take a swipe at passersby. I did not know that this might signal a personality disorder of the First Magnitude.

The first thing Sam did when he reached his new home was hide in a woodpile for a week. It wasn't even our woodpile! My parents took one look at this cat, a blue-tip Siamese with papers which had cost me a pretty penny, and promptly gave it away. But I turned the traditional legacy of parents to children around, guilt ("the gift that keeps on giving") and convinced them that Sam should be allowed to stay. It took Rick Roehrkasse, his temporary owner, about three days to get Sam out of the woodpile and return him to my parents.

As a pet, you want a cat that endears himself to you, twining through your legs in the kitchen upon your return from work or jumping into your lap to be petted and scratched before a roaring fire, purring contentedly. Sam seemed to have adopted the maxim, "Neither a twiner nor a purrer be."

Next time I get a cat, I will put out a job description first. The cats I have owned prefer hiding in woodpiles or furnaces, emitting inhuman noises which are grating to the ear, and breaking things. None of my cats even "meowed" in the traditional sense of the word. They sounded like Mingo from the planet Mercury.

One night, Sam began yowling from the basement bedroom in the wee hours of the morning. There was a clothes chute that went directly from my parents' bedroom to the basement where Sam slept at night. Finally, Dad had had enough! He decided to try a little behavior modification.

Dad attached a long clothesline to Sam's collar. Every time Sam let out with a blood-curdling yowl, Dad yanked on the cord. Picture my father, lying there in bed, yanking away like a crazed weasel. Cruel as it may sound, the alternative, at this point, for Sam was a trip to the vet and the ultimate trip to Paw Print Gardens, that cemetery for deceased felines.

When Dad went to the basement to release Sam the next morning, the Siamese cat shot out of that basement as though he were jet-propelled! Right behind him was the foreign cat interloper that had *really* been making all this noise. Cat Number Two had apparently climbed in through the basement window and had been hiding behind the furnace all along. Dad had been jerking the wrong cat's chain all night long! (Insert your own "jerking your chain" joke here.)

Sam had always been cross-eyed, a characteristic of the breed, but you can bet that *this* morning, he was more cross than cross-eyed!

Safe Sex?

From Monmouth, Illinois, we have the story of a Galesburg man who crossed the center line and crashed head-on into an oncoming truck, killing his female companion.

Sonny S. M—-, age 32, was found guilty on May 9, 2003, of aggravated driving under the influence. His female companion, Christina V——, who was killed in the January 17, 2002 accident, was found with the steering wheel embedded in her back, naked from the waist down.

The two had been driving from Scooters' Cabaret, a strip club in Gladstone, Illinois, to their home in Galesburg. Although the two were not dating, they had been living together with Mr. M—'s ex-wife. Mr. M—- was found outside the 1990 Chevy Caprice, his pants and underwear down around his ankles, wearing a condom.

Here's the part I don't get: the guy is using a condom. Usually, this is a sign of "safe sex." However, while he is having sex, Mr. M— is hurtling 60 to 65 miles per hour down U.S. Highway 34, between Biggsville (I'm not making that up) in Henderson County, and Kirkwood in Warren County (Illinois). Is this "safe sex" or a bizarre version of some sort of sexual demolition derby?

James Mueller, a truck driver for Sara Lee Bread Company, was following "about 12 to 15 car lengths" behind Mr. M—, and described the Chevy Caprice as "driving erratically."

I would think so. I'm still trying to figure out how he was driving at all. Mr. Mueller, one of the eyewitnesses at the trial, described the M— car as reaching speeds of 60 to 65 miles per hour and then dropping back to 30 to 35 miles per hour.

The Caprice crossed the centerline and hit a 1999 Freightline truck nearly head-on, about 5:20 a.m., four miles east of the Henderson County line.

I served on two coroners' juries in Rock Island County in Illinois. Unlike other states, in Illinois a jury of regular folk like me have to decide whether a person involved in a fatal accident is guilty of several charges. If the death is ruled a homicide or accidental or if negligence is found by the jury, it can make a difference in whether insurance pays off to the family.

Reckless homicide was one of the charges dropped in Mr. M—'s case, when the state failed to prove its case that he was high on marijuana at the time of the accident. Although Mr. M—'s blood alcohol level was .06 (below the legally intoxicated limit of .08 in Illinois) there was evidence of THC, a component of cannabis, in his urine.

Let's all keep in mind, while driving, that the person driving the other car might be Sonny M—.

And we know what that means.

The Bar Czar

A friend of ours who fancies himself an entrepreneur we have dubbed "the Bar Czar," in honor of one of his schemes: joint ownership of a bar. That project was fairly ordinary by the Bar Czar's standards.

Some of his schemes, like his fleet of chimney sweeps, his home-designed and produced sailboat (despite never having been a sailor), or his Bunkie Hunt buy-up-silver phase were amusing. The sailboat (he had never sailed, nor did he know anyone who sailed) soon gave way to a project involving the making and selling of religious icons. Then, he had an idea involving local publicity for others by mailing things from home.

There was also the photoelectric cell, which was designed to trigger lights from outside a building, for use whenever police drove by, to check a vacant supermarket or liquor store. This, he figured, was a foolproof crime deterrent, as the lights would come on as the cops cruised by. It never saw the light of day.

I thought of the entrepreneurial tendencies in my own family. Dad once had the opportunity to buy Winnebago stock at the very beginning of the company. He chose, instead, to invest in a Canadian mutual fund which had the distinction of being the only mutual fund that year to founder on the rocks of capitalism.

Mother decreed, in her infinite wisdom, that TV was "just a fad." Her exact words were, "Pictures were never meant to fly through the air." She invested, instead, in a copper mine in Bolivia that was soon confiscated by the government. Mother's feeling that TV was a passing fad explains why I had to watch "Captain Video and his Video Rangers" at Leah Hunter's house next door all those years ago, to see Tobor the Robot do his thing. We didn't have a television set until I was in high school, long after everyone else owned one.

Mother always claimed to have predicted Pearl Harbor days in advance and, therefore, thought that all her predictions were right on target. (No pun intended).

Commenting on the family tradition of dabbling in economic disaster, I was advised by my broker to buy tax-free municipal bonds when what I, a movie buff, really wanted to do was to invest in a movie production firm called Delphi I.

After I followed the "safe" course of action outlined by my broker and invested in the bonds, Delphi I—that fly-by-night investment opportunity that my broker advised me against—made money hand over fist with 38% ownership of the blockbuster movie "Tootsie."

I also must own up to buying LTV Steel stock just before that company went totally bankrupt, taking 6,000 employees in Ohio,

Indiana, and Illinois down with it. Worse yet, my son was one of those employees.

I used to make fun of the Bar Czar's schemes, with chimney sweeps, sailboats and religious icons, but the other day he confided that he had never lost money on an investment. With my family's track record in money management, maybe he knows something we don't know.

The only time I've been right, so far, was when I told my incredulous broker at Baird that I was going to sell both my businesses, because George "W" Bush had just been elected. (Or so said the Supreme Court and Florida.)

"Andy, " I said, "he'll ruin the economy and get us into a war." So, I sold two businesses that were going well to write this stuff for you.

Three wars and one Big Recession later (not to mention the $5 a gallon gas headed our way), I rest my case.

Sometimes, maybe we don't do too badly, since that was 2002 and my predictions for that AND the Toyota Prius were right on the money.

From the "Truth is Stranger than Fiction" File

Recently, a local radio station (KBOB) offered anyone who would agree to have the station's call letters tattooed on their foreheads $150,000 apiece. Or so say David Winkleman of Davenport and his twenty-one-year-old step-son, Richard Goddard, Jr. The two men talked to station representatives and then proceeded to have KBOB tattooed across their foreheads. This made them into walking billboards for the station.

After that, things went horribly awry. The station reneged on the alleged monetary award, claiming that was not the offer. Mr. Goddard lost his job and said that he could not find other employment because he had KBOB tattooed on his forehead. A civil lawsuit was filed by Mr. Goddard against the radio station, but he failed to appear for his January 31, 2003 deposition, or another motion for a hearing on February 13, 2003.

Somehow, Mr. Goddard ended up living in the Kershaw Trailer Park in Colona, Illinois, with John and Mary Rushman, 47 and 44. I assume they were friends at one time. Mr. Goddard complained so much about his bad luck that his hosts decided to "teach him a lesson" by stringing him up in their trailer by throwing a rope over a low-hanging ceiling beam. (With friends like these, who needs enemies?)

Here is where things get sticky. I once read a Janet (Harridan) Daily romance novel where her plot has a horse being hung. At the point in the plot where the bad guys are stringing up the horse, I had to stop and think about the logistics of hanging a horse in a barn. I must admit that I never could figure out how that was possible. I did not recover sufficiently to read the rest of the book.

Along those same lines, I am still thinking about most trailers I am aware of and wondering…ceiling beams? My impression of most trailers is that they are not very tall structures. But, hey! I've never been to the Rushmans' trailer, and, with any luck, I never will have that unforgettable experience. I still wonder how you can hang someone inside a trailer. Indeed, perhaps you cannot, because Mr. Goddard is still alive and kicking, although he did have to spend two nights in a local hospital.

The Rushmans, always the perfect hosts, also beat David Goddard, Jr., with a ball-peen hammer while trying to hang him. Mrs. Goddard (Mary) is charged with aggravated battery for allegedly hitting Mr. Goddard in the right arm with the hammer while Goddard was wrestling with her husband John.

Mr. Rushman (John) was charged with aggravated battery for allegedly hitting Mr. Goddard in the face with the hammer, a second count of aggravated battery for attempting to hang David Goddard, a third count of aggravated battery for allegedly pushing a police officer, and one count of criminal damage to state property for kicking the window out of a Colona police car. A misdemeanor count of resisting arrest was filed against Mr. Rushman.

Both of the Rushmans have pleaded guilty to the charges. They were scheduled to appear for a pre-trail hearing on July 17, 2003. Hopefully, no one around them will complain too much, in the future.

What have we learned from this news story, boys and girls? Don't listen to radio stations that advertise big bucks if you will do something stupid, because the station might not pay off? Never try to hang something or someone in a structure that isn't tall enough? Don't drink while around someone with KBOB tattooed on his (or her) forehead? Don't complain if you *have* KBOB tattooed on your forehead?

I'm not sure what the lesson to be learned is, but I am sure there is one.

The 1984 Olympics

I had a rather unique Olympic experience in 1984. After watching one-half of the Olympics in Los Angeles on television in the United States, right through Mary Lou Retten's vaulting medal, I watched the last half on television in West Germany, Sweden, Denmark and Norway.

One obvious problem with watching a program broadcast in not one, but four languages I do not speak, was my inability to understand what the expert commentators were saying.

A race is still a race, though, and, after reading some scathing British commentary in the London press about our United States coverage by ABC, I wasn't sure I had missed that much.

British columnist Julian Barnes, who specializes in television criticism for the London *Daily Mail*, wrote an article in which he reported experiences similar to my own, as he had watched the first half of the Olympics in Texas, on American television (ABC) and the second half of the competition in London on the BBC.

Among criticisms leveled at ABC's announcers and reporters, he described veteran anchorman Jim McKay as "a stumbling, blue-jacketed droner" and denounced the American athletes used as commentators, who, he said, fell short of their task by "letting out

Apache war whoops as their sole analytic comment on a compatriot's performance." [Ah, those wacky Brits!]

Barnes was properly aghast at the ABC commentator who solemnly informed us, as one bicyclist closely tailed another, "The one who's not in front is breaking a lot of wind." Barnes also didn't think much of John Williams' "Olympic Anthem." His exact words were, 'If you find the 'Chariots of Fire' theme moany and obvious, you haven't been subjected to John Williams' 'Olympic Anthem' 24 times or so an hour, before and after each commercial break."

Barnes hated the opening ceremony. "BBC viewers, unlike ABC viewers, were spared the ABC subtitles during the opening march past of contestants, which explained the size and location of each competing country. Not just with Bhutan ('location: Central Asia; size: approximately ½ Indiana') but with Belgium ('in NW Europe') and Bangladesh ('approximately the size of Wisconsin.').

Harsh words from this British critic! We might also say, "Them's fightin' words", which, as I recall, Americans did say to the British, circa 1776, with interesting results.

But let me return to my original topic and tell you what it was like watching the Olympics on foreign soil. The question,

"How long can you tread water?" might be rephrased as, "How long can you watch the Swedish two-woman kayak races?" Or, the West German women's fencing team? The event that seemed to be of the most interest to these viewers was the celebrated decathlon duel between West Germany's Jurgen Hidsen ("the German Hercules") and Britain's Daley Thompson, which Thompson won. That is what I saw, and that is *all* I saw.

Carl Lewis was strictly, "Carl who?" in Denmark. I saw re-runs of the West German women's fencers taking the gold and falling over backwards in happiness afterwards fully seven times in one hour, on television in Munich. After a few evenings which consisted solely of watching obscure events won by the Danes, Germans, Swedes and Norwegians, I was glad to be able to switch to "From Here to Eternity" and James Dean in "Rebel Without a Cause," even though both were dubbed in German, which I do not speak or understand. Still, it was an improvement. I was reminded of the time that my husband had said I would be a perfect candidate for the "Forward 100-Meter Roll," [which, for all I know, is a real event.]

Perhaps the attitude of Europeans I encountered was best summed up by my former Swedish student at Augustana College, Per Olof Gustaffsson, who flipped off his set in the middle of yet another cranking out of "Oh Say Can You See?" saying good-naturedly, "U.S. smashes the rest of the world. Bo-ring!"

To this American and many others, it was NOT boring. There is a resurgence of patriotism abroad in our land. The United States had a fantastic Olympics and, at the risk of being proclaimed an ugly American, I'm not afraid to tell the world.

However, I still could be amused by critics like Julian Barnes, and I enjoyed this anecdote he told, praising a British broadcaster named David Coleman.

"The games did throw up a few jollies. My favorite moment came at some eyelid-dropping time on Tuesday morning, when an American girl won the 400 meters. The habitual mayhem ensued, 'And there she is in the arms of her boyfriend,' exclaimed BBC sportscaster David Coleman warmly."(The incident referred to happened when Valerie Brisco-Hooks embraced her husband, Alvin Sr., after winning the Women's 400-meter race).

Coleman continued: "But by then the camera had panned across to the embrace. The man was lying splay-legged on his back and the gold medallist herself was atop him in what is usually referred to as the female missionary position. After a few moments, they rolled over and showed us the other way."

Coleman, understandably stumped for words, lunged for his mental fact file on the winner. What he came up with was this, "And she's got a 2-year-old son, Alvin Jr.!"

Concluded Barnes (on Coleman), "I shouldn't think a viewer in this land was at all surprised."

Al Franken and Me:
Jefferson/Jackson
Democratic Dinner in Des Moines, 2004

Keynote Speaker – Al Franken

AND YOU ARE THERE!

Or

"A Mush Mute, a Big Hat and a Plum"

Just a few comments about the October 16th Jefferson/Jackson annual Democratic dinner at Veterans' Memorial Auditorium in Des Moines.

1) The acoustics at Veterans' Memorial Auditorium suck.

2) Because the acoustics suck, the large TV screens have captioning. The captioning must be done by a machine. This can lead to much merriment. Especially if you have made it your goal, after at least three hours of waiting, to obtain and consume a minimum of three glasses of white zinfandel prior to Al Franken's appearance as the keynote speaker.

3) "Ed is the Governor of Pencil." I think the machine MEANT to say that Ed is or was the Governor of Pennsylvania.

4) The word "Dear" is listed as "Deer."

5) The machine cannot make up its mind whether the choir of Gospel Singers is from the Maple or Elm Street Missionary Baptist Church Choir. At this point, the machine is introducing various tree types. Things are very confused.

6) We are asked to join hands with the person next to us. The person next to me, on my right, is Thomas Fischermann, Economic Correspondent for the German weekly "Die Zeit." I tell Tom that holding hands in this fashion in America means that we are now legally married. Tom tells me that he knows this isn't true, as he was raised Catholic. I admit that I lied (which is more than I can say for George W. Bush). Tom turns out to be a delightful seat-mate for the dinner, which we are not eating.

7) At one point, after the droning of fully two dozen would-be Democratic candidates, none of whom any of us knows, Tom says he might have to go back to his hotel room and watch Al (Franken) on TV. (He doesn't.) He is disappointed that Sharon Stone isn't going to appear (Aren't we all?) I ask Tom whether he thinks Vanessa Kerry is wearing nylons. He is too much of a gentleman to comment. [Oh, those European men. Especially those who had English teachers from Wisconsin.]

8) After about 2 hours of the droning and bellering (the sound system is *REALLY* bad), I say that it is going to be my goal to drink three glasses of white zinfandel before Franken takes the stage. I am

actually doubting that Franken will EVER take the stage. This turns out to be a really bad plan. Why?

I have taken my college roommate as photographer-in-residence, and, when I put my camera and the wine glasses (small plastic cups at $5 per glass) on the floor, she accidentally kicks a glass of white zinfandel over my camera. It completely soaks it. Thomas rescues the camera from the ever-widening pool of wine. The strap is soaked. The lens is "cloudy." I do not get one single usable picture from my trusty Canon after the unfortunate wine incident, henceforth known as "Zinfandel-gate." As I did manage to secure two glasses of zinfandel prior to Zinfandel-gate, I don't care. Later, I will rue the day. Or night.

9) To my extreme left is Jane, correspondent for *People* magazine. Jane is covering the candidate's children for a story. Jane is very nice. She is dressed in black. She would like some food. We do not get any food. We would not get anything to drink, either, if I hadn't made the infamous "Zinfandel-gate" run. (*Kids: Take note! Do NOT try this at home!)

10) Other errors on the sub-title machine that amuse me: "Fill" for a candidate whose first name is "Phil." "He is a man of grass." (This may actually be accurate; we don't know. Perhaps he meant that "W" is an ass? Or a man of ass? Very confusing. Don't know; can't tell you.)

11) When someone says, "The future of this country is at stake. The future of the world is at stake," Thomas leans over and says, "The

sky is falling." I laugh. Perhaps I should write this down? Again, don't know; can't tell you.

12) More machine sub-title errors: for "pirate suit," (which is connected to Al Franken's remarks about George W. Bush wearing a ridiculous flight suit with a huge cod-piece on his now-infamous "Mission Accomplished" battleship appearance). The machine spells out: "pie rat."

Perhaps this machine is smarter than anyone realizes.

13) Other errors that I cannot explain, from the sub-titling machine: "sash and acute" (?) "A mush mute, a big hat and a plum."

14) I enjoyed Al Franken's remark that, after 9/11, the country was very united. "My college roommate even got out an old T-shirt to wear that touted America. Of course, it took him four hours to white-out 'sucks.'"

15) What have I learned from this experience? Never trust sub-titling machines. Always trust the German correspondent for "Die Zeit." He is very knowledgable, very handsome, and we chat at great length about the Diebolt voting machines and the potential for voter fraud in the upcoming election. Please give Thomas a raise; I think he likes Vanessa Kerry, and he will need it to win her heart.

16) Never try to drink three glasses of white zinfandel while simultaneously shooting film and taking notes. But it's ok to laugh. A lot.

Intrepid Reporter Covers Dubuque Rally

Blog for Iowa (Aug. 3, 2004)

When I received the tickets to attend John Kerry's Dubuque, Iowa, appearance on August 3, 2004, from MoveOn.org, I made the mistake of telling the daughter that Dave Grohl of the Foo Fighters would be appearing with Kerry. Even though Kerry and crowd were scheduled to hit our home town area the very same night, nothing would do but that we take best friend Amanda Burkert and hit the road for Dubuque, some 60 miles to the north.

What follows is an hour-by-hour re-telling of the successful rally, which, they say, drew 4,700 people. (The fire marshall quit letting people into the Center after about 1,000, so this must be the estimate derived from the number of tickets pre-printed off the internet or collected at the door.)

It is the first day of school for the daughter and her companion, Amanda, and it is only August 3rd. United Township High School in East Moline, Illinois, has gone to a year-round schedule this year. Result: the girls sleep all the way on the hour-long drive to Dubuque.

3:00 p.m. – We arrive, park, and walk to the venue for the rally, which is the Dubuque Five Flags Center, changed from the outdoor Watchtower Plaza. Button-vendors approach us. I agree to pay $10 for 3 buttons, but only the "clean" ones. I select "John-John 2004" for myself. One girl selects "Cute Chicks Go for Edwards" while the other picks "If You Can Read This, You Aren't the President." However, there are other more "colorful" buttons (one reads BU—SH__) which I refuse to purchase for the under-age girls, who promptly whip out their OWN money and buy them, anyway, as well as the "Asses of Evil" one.

3:30 p.m. – It turns out that we have been waiting at the wrong door. It works out well for Amanda, who is interviewed by Channel 7 regarding her opinion of rock artists campaigning for their favorite candidates. Amanda is wearing pink glasses that make her look like she is auditioning for a remake of "Return from the Black Lagoon." They are thick, goggle-like, and pink plastic. We have been kidding her about these glasses all day. She looks darling! The girls look very cute. This has not escaped the young reporter's attention. (Nobody wants to ask me anything.) When asked why she is in attendance, Amanda says, "My friend's mother made me come." I had predicted a 9:00 p.m. return home, while we really don't back until 11:00 p.m. on a school night! Sorry, Amanda's mom.

4:00 p.m. -We begin chatting with those around us, who are now beginning to pass out. ("MEDIC! MEDIC!") I am not kidding about the passing out. It is very hot and sultry out. The first person collapses at 4:10 p.m. There are many people in wheelchairs, being wheeled by relatives, and the high humidity, high temperatures, threat of thunderstorms, and tornado warnings contribute to a really miserable in-line experience. I learn that the young couple behind us have driven from Oelwein, Iowa, which is at least a 3-hour drive. The woman from Savannah, Illinois pushing the elderly woman in the wheelchair has the only "local" in tow who is actually from Dubuque.

4:15 p.m. - We begin chatting with the couple immediately ahead of us, John and Mary from Dysart, Iowa. John has a pace-maker and Mary has a device to help with back-pain (electric signals to pained spine). We become fast friends and, when the door-keepers offer to let the wheelchair-bound and less-than-healthy inside the air-conditioned lobby area, we immediately say, "We're with them!" Mary comments that Bush is "Just a bonehead" and that, with Bush, it is always "my way or the highway." (Hear, hear!) Mary and I exchange phone numbers and I tell her about www.blogforiowa, but she doesn't have a computer. John is upset that he is expected to go through security (the pace-maker can't be scanned) and the wait is going to be long. (Four hours, to be exact). He tells Mary that this will be his last rally. A wise man.

4:45 p.m. – We are now inside the auditorium, which is nearly empty at this point, as everyone goes through extensive metal detector screening. We get really good seats: cushioned, not too far from the stage. Nobody is there yet. They examine my cell phone and camera, as I go through the screening line, as though they expect them to actually DO something other than make phone calls and take pictures. This takes at least 10 minutes. My purse is so large that a small family could live inside it. The billfold falls open and change hits the ground. There are thousands of people who are going to have to go through this drawn-out, laborious procedure. They should have started the security at 2:00 p.m., I'm thinking.

The musical selections that we are listening to seem to be the exact same soundtrack recently heard at the Democratic convention, i.e., "Livin' in the USA" (James Brown); Bruce Springsteen;" I Feel Good"; "Shout! "(from "Animal House").

5:00 p.m. – Stacey announces that she needs to use the rest room. She is reluctant to ask the Secret Service man (who is extremely nice to us all evening) where it is. Finally, she does ask, and learns that it is just up the stairs and on the landing. The girls are hungry, although we ate right before leaving town. (Teen-agers!)

5:10 p.m. – Songs we are listening to (and listening to and listening to): "Love Train"; "Right Here, Right Now" (Jesus Jones);" I'm a Believer" (the Monkees);" It's A Beautiful Day" (U2). I mention this only in light of the recent news of the rock stars who are going to attempt to help us unseat the incumbent.

Go, Bruce and Friends! GREAT idea! Sign me up!

5:20 p.m. – I talk with the friendly Secret Service agent, who tells me that the Kerry party has been "delayed" in Beloit, Wisconsin, and that they probably won't arrive in Dubuque until at least 7:00 p.m. (AAARRRGGHHH!!) A woman directly behind me says, "I can't believe all the kids here!" What does she think is the draw? Does she know who the Foo Fighters are? Will there be Kung Fu Fighting? No foo, no kids. Whether the Foo Fighters themselves are actually going to fight....errr, play, is still up in the air. Registration of young voters is the order of the day outside the auditorium. This idea might really work, I'm thinking.

5:30 p.m. - Several dignitaries are identified in the crowd, including Tom Miller, the Attorney General; Tom Harkin, our U.S. Senator (and former ardent Dean supporter); and Tom Vilsack (the Governor of Iowa.). It seems that, if you don't know someone's name, just calling them "Tom" will suffice. (My son had a wedding party like that, only the name, then, was "Chris.") Sally Pederson, the Lieutenant Governor of the state takes the stage and says a few words, as does Bill Gluba, who is running for office (and, in 2011, is Mayor of Davenport, Iowa). A VFW member (Troop 9683) leads us in the Pledge of Allegiance.

5:50 p.m. – A weathered-looking roadie enters and begins tuning the guitar for Dave Grohl. The kids in the front (who will later mouth every word of every song that Grohl sings) become very excited. The "tuning" process seems to consist mainly of saying "Yeah, yeah, yeah.

Hey, hey. Check, check, check." At one point he asks, "Do you have separate house and monitor controls?" When the response is "yes," he says, "Cool. Thanks, man," and leaves.

6:00 p.m. - Music is now Sousa's "Stars & Stripes Forever," followed by Tina Turner's "Better Than All the Rest." Bill Gluba's rousing remarks are that Bush has "Virtually ignored the middle class." Gluba is politely received. Tom Harkin takes the stage and says, "We need to fully support our veterans when they come home from this war." Today, in 2011, we might legitimately ask, "Which war?" Harkin's remark gets a big round of applause, and he pumps up the crowd by saying, "Bush is going down! Kerry's going up! That's the way God meant it to be! Like father, like son: one term and he's done! What we need in the White House is an OAK, not a Bush!" (*If Harkin had been right, we might not have a record debt of $14 trillion in 2011.)

6:15 p.m. - Harkin is followed by the Governor and Mrs. Vilsack. The Governor comments that Harkin is "a hard act to follow," which proves to be true. The Governor repeats, "It's time for a change!" He remarks that there are now 14 Iowa kids dead in the Iraq war. "It is time to bring America back to where it once was - a stronger and more respected America." He applauds his wife's speech at the recent Democratic convention in Boston. (*Revisiting this in 2011, one wonders how many Iowa kids are now dead in the Iraq War. A lot more than 14, when you factor in Afghanistan, et. al.)

6:30 p.m. – Dave Grohl takes the stage and plays "Learn to Fly" on acoustic guitar. (I'm lookin' to the sky to save me….lookin' for a sign of life…..lookin' for something to help me burn out bright…" The song contains the line "Make my way back home when I learn to fly.") The kids love it. Grohl is one of the most convincing speakers all night.

Dave Grohl tells the crowd that it was brought to his attention that the Bush camp was using HIS songs. He did not like that. He says that he has been in bands for 18 years and is now 35 years old (and married, girls. Sorry.) "I have traveled all over the world, and always before, when I would meet a person in Russia or Shanghai or Africa, they would reach out their hand to shake mine and they were happy to meet an American. Now, under George W. Bush, that feeling is gone. I want that feeling back." He follows up these remarks with the song "Times Like These" ("I found a new day risin'…I'm a little divided…to stay or run away…Leave it all behind…It's times like these you learn to live again…") When they asked him if he would stump with Kerry, he asked if there was a stage. When the answer was "yes," he said, "If you build it, I will come." (Good line for Dubuque, where "Field of Dreams" was filmed in nearby Dyersville.)

6:45 p.m. - Greg and Kelly Simpson and their family of six kids (one of whom, Madison, her mother forgets during the introductions) take the stage with John and Teresa Kerry. The Simpsons have worked very hard for Kerry in Dubuque. One of their older teen-aged daughters was a Democratic delegate in Boston. All the kids wear tee shirts of their own designs, with slogans like, "Maddy Reporting for Duty" and "Believe in America." I wonder how Maddy feels about her mother forgetting to mention her name. I wonder if "the Simpsons" from Dubuque are related to TV's Simpsons.

7:00 p.m. - – Teresa Kerry talks. And talks. And talks. She likes to talk and has a lot of opinions. Does the woman talk a tad too much? (I should know; it takes one to know one.)

Finally, Teresa turns the microphone over to her husband, the candidate, and Kerry delivers a speech that is much more biting than others delivered previously, especially on the subjects of Iraq and the economy. He introduces Andre Heinz, his step-son, and seems at ease and much more "energetic" than he did during the last speech I heard him give at the Davenport Radisson, during the Iowa caucuses, when he was nursing a sore throat and had a number of his veteran buddies with him. He hits most of the same themes that he hit during the Democratic convention in Boston. At the end, there is a flurry of confetti that drops from the ceiling. It is like a "Mini-Boston."

I quit taking notes, because I am now shooting film (2 rolls). Therefore, each and every word is not recorded for posterity because I give this task to the girls and they fail miserably at their appointed task. ("What? You wanted us to write something down?") At one point, I look back to take a shot of the girls in their seats, and they are holding their "Believe in America" signs upside down. My daughter put her gum under her chair. Then, she got the gum all over her jeans. I am not sure whether I am more upset that she would stick her gum under a chair or that she just got it all over her new jeans. A motherly lecture ensues. Luckily, at this point in time she is selling clothes at Pacific Sunwear at Southpark Mall and can replace the jeans at a discount. She is quite upset, as these are her "favorite jeans." I tell her about the ice cube/knife trick, and she immediately tries it in our booth DURING DINNER. (Gack!) I tell her NOT to use the knife she just scraped gum off her jeans with to eat with. She gives me a withering look.

I am in a very good spot for shooting film, and I am enjoying the rally. Nobody is thrown to the ground and frisked, as happens the next day at the Bush rally at Davenport's LeClaire Park, but we did have old people hitting the ground during the long wait outside in stifling heat. (Luckily, I was not one of the old people hitting the ground, but never say never).

We know it is raining outside and that there are tornado warnings out for the area. (Either that, or the Secret Service guys are REALLY working up a sweat!) We are warm and dry in the arena, however, and, by the time the rally is over,…. which is hours later… it is only sprinkling outside. The girls use their "Believe in America" posters to cover their heads as we walk the two blocks to the car, but I only have my notebook. (The one that has no notes written in it after 7:00 p.m. Thanks, Girls!)

We adjourn to a nearby "brewery" and restaurant which has excellent food and service. The girls have school in the morning, so we must drive home ASAP. (The daughter is now doing the ice cube/knife trick. I am sure she will poke a hole in the new jeans with the steak knife she is using.)

An incoming call from the husband, at home in the Illinois Quad Cities, notifies us that he is sitting in the dark listening to his transistor radio, as power has failed in the Quad Cities. We have experienced none of that, although a light rain falls as we drive home. We arrive by 11:00 p.m. I tell the daughter to take all proof of her civic activity to her Government class, which she promises to do, but then does not do. (Typical).

*****Over and Out from your www.blogforiowa.com correspondent, Connie Corcoran Wilson. Next time, PRESS CREDENTIALS, I'm thinking. What do you say to that?*****

Connie Corcoran Wilson

The Daughter and The Road Trip

Connie submits this report from her cross-state Democratic Road Trip
with "the daughter." (Ames, IA Dave Matthews Band Concert)

The daughter and I returned from our SIX-HOUR concert on
campus at Iowa State University in Ames, Iowa about 1:30 a.m. last
night. I cannot remember a concert where I drew Snoopy on the left
ankle of the young man behind me in red ink and then, on his right
ankle, played tic-tac-toe with my daughter. (It was a draw.) Plus, I
sprayed BOTH of the young man's feet with Burberry perfume (from
my purse) since they were really smelly feet, which he insisted on
parking on the arms of *MY* chair.

At one point, he grabbed my notebook and wrote in it, "I have no
idea what you are doing here. I can't see shit, but keep this. Thanks
and bye." Earlier, I heard the young man and his friends discussing
how I "probably remembered every President back to Lincoln." The
sad thing is, they are right. He kids me about "growing up in the
seventies" and wants to know if I ever "smoked reefer." I feel flattered
that he thinks I "grew up in the 70's." That makes me younger than I
really am, so I am enjoying that comment. As for the reefer question:

allergic, you know. Only contact highs. I respond, "Yes, but I never inhaled," thinking he will get the joke. He does not.

In the parking lot afterwards, while waiting for the cars to move out to the road, the car ahead of us contains a fake snake. One of the young college men in the party puts the snake between his legs and gyrates like a Chippendale Dancer. The snake looks very real, so I roll my car windows up. The daughter, who is beginning to sound a little like Typhoid Mary, asks, "Why are you rolling up the windows?" I pretend it is for her health. It is really because I fear that the kid with the snake might gyrate over to us and do God-knows-what.

Neil Young (of the old group Crosby, Stills, Nash and Young) comes onstage at one point with the Dave Matthews Band and plays (a "surprise" performance). My notes, at that point: "They are holding this guitar note for so long that pain will soon ensue. They are all watching Neil, for a 'sign.' He has, apparently, forgotten the sign. I am beginning to think that the "sign" is that your ears begin to bleed. Neil looks like Howard Hughes on a bad day. He is engaged in some sort of guitar death throe. Some blonde woman comes onstage with him, but I don't think anyone has a clue who she is (I know I don't). I ask, but the boys behind me have passed out, and nobody else can hear me over the guitar punishment. Yikes!

The new camera (Olympus digital), which was fully charged before the concert, only ran for 2 hours. The concert lasted 6. [Thank God for my trusty old Canon, pre-Zinfandel gate]. The daughter got pictures of "My Morning Jacket," "Jurassic5," and "Ben Harper and the Innocent Criminals," but where was my digital camera when the Main Act came onstage? Why, dead, of course. As I fear I will be after this six-hour marathon.

At one point, Ben Harper plays a song called "Burn One Down," which either has to do with forest fires or smoking marijuana. Other lyrics I hear, but don't know: "Kick your butt." "Plastic." "Fuck the president." "I always have to steal my kisses from you." "This is a song about freedom. There's some people who smoke a lot of weed, cause some of those [bleep] haven't gotten off the couch for two years. Then, that [bleep] wanders out in to the street holdin' his remote and gettin' his groove on. If you ain't where you want to be in your life, put the bong down, Homey." This brings on "Burn One Down," which seems to involve a haze of illegal smoke. "Your choice is who you choose to be. We are gonna' burn one down."

Good to see that our college students are becoming more articulate every day. Gives one hope. I hope they don't burn anything down while I am inside it.

Back to lyrics: "No lives for bullshit—." "He offered life in sacrifice, so others could go on." Neil Young sings (if you can call it that), "It was just a legend. War was never known. The people were together, and they lifted many stones." I'm thinking this might be "Along the Watchtower," but I really am not "in" to Neil Young. He looks like television's the Crypt-Keeper.

None of the young kids there know who he is, or who the old blonde with him is. Then there is something about dancing across the water. Neil seems somewhat uncoordinated, so I don't think he will be doing any dancing across water or any other surface any time soon. It is as though Bigfoot has been taking guitar lessons and has been unleashed upon us.

I know three songs all night long, including the Dave Matthews Band encore song "Too Much" from the "Crash" album; "Keep on Rockin' in the USA" and a version of Buffalo Springfield's, "There's somethin' happenin' here; Stop, Baby! What's that sound? Everybody look what's goin' down." This is repeated about 20 times. I remember it was used in a documentary about the Vietnam War that I used to show my 7th grade students.

At one point, trying to be friendly, I say, to the black guy next to me, "I took her to her first Dave Matthews Band concert when he had "Under the Table and Dreaming" out. She was ten." The guy says, "Oh. Yeah. I remember that concert. I passed out halfway through it."

O.........K.

Now, Neil plays TAPS on his guitar. Why? We don't know. Dave and the others are sort of glassy-eyed, mesmerized, staring at Neil. This concert has lasted a Looooong time. Someone please make Neil quit!!! The drunk guys from St. Joseph's, Missouri, or Joplin, Missouri have all passed out, which is when and why I draw Snoopy on one of their ankles.

The girl ahead of me is wildly flailing her arms like a windmill. Too much caffeine, I'm thinking. This girl is known, henceforth, as "Hyperactive Girl," or HG. Every time I try to take a shot, she pumps her fist in the air just as I shoot. I have a lot of photos of her fist(s)

As usual, I attempt to pick out "bobbleheads" in the arena. These are people who are making absolute fools of themselves. My God! This must be the Bobblehead Convention. The violin guy onstage is going nuts, and the guy wearing the Number One jersey with the page boy bob haircut is doing something that I can only describe as NOT likely to impress anyone.

The drunk or stoned guy behind me ("Max", says his NAME TAG) keeps trying to bump my arm as I take notes, and, at one point, he actually tries to relieve me of my notebook. But I'm too quick for him. (Catlike quickness).

Ms. Hyperactive is now resorting to rabbit-like punching in the air. The guy she is with is very tall and looks like the one who once played Claire's boyfriend Russell on "Six Feet Under." He is wearing a shirt that says "America's Music Festival to End All Festivals" while his girlfriend has on a "Farm Aid, September 18th" shirt. I fear for Ms. Hyperactive's safety, as she is so out-of-control that I think she is going to fall over the balcony railing any minute.

Neil (Young) is doing some kind of geriatric jig. Someone make Neil quit. Please.

Republican Women Don't Flush

(10/25/04)

Considering that one of the Republican bumper stickers bears the message "Flush the Johns," I learned something surprising at the Bush rally at the Davenport, Iowa, River Center on Monday, October 25th, 2004. Republican women don't flush. At least, not as much as they should. Three stalls on the left side of the rest room. Only one was flushed. [Please join me in a chorus of "Eeeuuuuwwww!"]

The crowd inside the River Center (Davenport, IA), which holds 4,000, was smaller than I had anticipated. At approximately 2/3 full, this would be 2,640 people. I later heard that only 3,000 tickets were distributed. The crowd was much smaller than that at the Edwards rally in Iowa City on Thursday, the 21st, and much smaller than that at the Waterloo airport for Kerry on Tuesday, October 19th.

I see numerous people I know on my way to the rally: my trust executive from Wells Fargo, the world's fifth-largest bank; Andrea Zinga and husband (who, since she is a Republican candidate from Illinois, running against Lane Evans, was surprisingly absent from the stage full of people-props behind Bush); Mary Jane and Rocky Nelson of Hampton, who worked for and with me for years at the Sylvan

Learning Center; Jane Robinson of Silvis, former Silvis School Board Member.

In other words, "the usual suspects," wonderful people all. But growing smaller and smaller in numbers, it seems. And, (with the exception of the above-mentioned account executive and the always-youthful Andrea), older and older. Not a one of them under seventy.

Bush rallies are full of people who are primarily....well.... old. (Takes one to know one.) Bush rallies usually seem to have many present who are better-dressed than their Democratic counterparts. Bush rallyers are more predictable, in that certain "buzz words" are used to denigrate the opposition and set off a Pavlovian response from the assembled mini-masses..."Flip-flop", for example, during this campaign year.

Republican rallies have Country & Western music or really old recorded music...and not much of that. At one point, I thought I heard a Rolling Stones song, but then, listening again, I thought: "Naaaaah." Republican rallies invoke God, over and over and over again. This makes me increasingly uneasy. (Whatever happened to "separation of church and state?")

Brian X., a candidate for the Iowa Senate, recited a prayer which went something like this: "We thank you for raising up a Commander-in-Chief who leads us so nobly. We are so inspired by his devotion to you. We pray you will grant him the ability to beat back our enemies." (*Note that it is "enemies," plural now. And growing by the minute!)

And, last but not least, there was something about "Hand of love, power, justice, and hope."

This time, unlike the Democratic rally at Vets Auditorium in Des Moines, we were not asked to actually join hands. Democrats must be more "hands on" people than Republicans.) After the rest room discovery, I was very relieved that I wasn't going to have to join hands with anyone. Especially not any of the non-flushing Republican women. [If they don't flush, do they wash?]

Next to me was Oliver, who writes for the British weekly *The Guardian* . I wondered what Oliver was thinking about this slice of Americana. I asked Oliver what he would be doing next.

He answered, "Lacrosse." I remember getting an e-mail from the Mark of the Quad Cities (now the I-Wireless Center), our civic center, about a lacrosse game and thinking, "Lacrosse? How-the-heck does lacrosse figure in Midwestern life?" This is what the traveling press will take away from visiting the Quad Cities: lacrosse. I leaned over and commented to Oliver, "Politics isn't like this in England, is it?" He agreed that it was not. At all. We talked about how religion is far less of an influence in British politics.

Actually, religion used to be far less of an influence in American politics, until the election of 2000 and the installation of "W's" fundamentalist group of "Christians." After that, we had John Ashcroft, our Attorney General, requiring his employees pray with him every morning in his office. (I repeat: "Whatever happened to separation of church and state?")

I don't remember "W"'s father (George Herbert) doing quite as much Bible-thumping as "W" every time he took the stage. (I do remember him throwing up in the Japanese Prime Minister's lap, but this is probably not the time to mention that unfortunate incident.) George Herbert seemed more reserved. Chilly, almost. Not like his hot-headed son, George, at all. I guess the apple does fall far from the tree.

A World War II veteran named Charles leads us forcefully in the Pledge of Allegiance. Nicole White (Miss Iowa) sings the National Anthem and really reaches up an octave for the high note, to the crowd's delight. Someone named Kim Franklin, who has a very nice voice, comes out to entertain the crowd during the very long wait and leads the crowd in singing "We Are Family" by Sister Sledge.

Correct me if I'm wrong, but wasn't that song popular in about 1979 or 1980? Amazon.com says, "This song doesn't just define the disco era, it transcends it." Sister Sledge has an 8-minute version, if you really want to re-visit the disco era. Personally, I am attempting to keep up with the 2000+ plus years. I never did well with platform shoes. Choosing this song to use at a Bush rally reinforces how out-of-touch "W"'s people are with the middle America of 2000 ...some 20 or 21 years after that song's release.

Before Kim appeared to sing, "live," we had Elvis' posthumous release "A Little Less Conversation," created from mixes the King left behind before he overdosed on August 16, 1977. An even older chestnut than "We Are Family", albeit one that was not released until years after the singer's death. (*Lyric: "A little less bite, a little more spark; Come on, baby, I'm tired of talkin' Grab your coat; let's do some walkin'".)

I was raised Catholic; I was a teen-ager when Kennedy was President...the last President I actively campaigned for, before now. Consider yourself slapped, E. [And that goes double for you, W]. Is this any kind of image for a "Compassionate Conservative" fundamentalist "Christian" to be promoting? Let's try to be CONSISTENT here, George. You can't have it both ways. Are you flip-flopping here, or just having a bad acid flashback to your college National Guard non-duty days?

Maggie Tinsman takes the podium and quotes Will Rogers: "Even when you're on the right track, you'll get run over if you just sit there." I'm not sure what this has to do with the election at all. It reminds me of the television ad that the Republicans are now running where a WTC victim's daughter comes out of her lethargy when "W" embraces her in a made-for-TV moment. Very convenient that the cameras were there to capture "W" doing his "compassionate conservative" bit. I wonder if there is similar footage of him cutting all those kids from after-school programs, Pell grants and Head Start programs.

I now (vaguely) remember George W. Bush making earlier political references to "tracks," and saying something on the campaign trail about how there were officials in Iraq who had said that they were on a better "track" there than we were here in the United States. If I were Ms. Tinsman I would find a better quote.

The tag team of John Kerry and John Edwards responded to the original "track" jibe by saying that the United States is on the WRONG track under George W. Bush, a refrain which many military men (among them Stansfield Turner, Director of the CIA from 1977 to 1981) echoed at the Waterloo rally at the Five Sullivan Brothers Center on Tuesday, October 19th. This "track" theme, on Ms. Tinsman's part, was probably ill-chosen. Maybe Republicans just like trains and can't think too critically about anything with a "track" reference. She ends quickly, endorsing Bush.

James Leach takes a much more statesmanlike turn at the microphone. He sounds almost professorial, urging us all to be less divided as a country during this hard-fought election. Hear, hear! He says that John Kerry is "a very credible standard bearer," but thinks that the Democratic Party, in general, has few good ideas. (*Interesting that James Leach will come around and actively work within the Obama Administration just 4 years later.)

Bombing Iraq back to the Stone Age, a Republican idea, was a "good" idea? And how about that "Crusade" comment by "W" that set the entire Arab world off on a "jihad" or Holy War against Americans? Also a Republican bone-head play. I'm thinking: NOT-so-"good," Mr. Leach. What about alienating all of the rest of the world? Can you say, "NOT good?") Mr. Leach repeats the refrain about electing "Laura Bush's husband," as though Laura Bush was the candidate here. (She's not, boys; get over it.)

Leach says that we should "Take a great country and make it better, not take a great country and talk it down." This echoes almost word-for-word the final lines of Edwards' speech in Iowa City on Thursday, October 21st, which he ended with these words, "The reason this election is so important is that we believe we should never look down on anyone. We should lift people up." Given the nearly identical words, Leach must be squarely behind John Edwards' candidacy. (Maybe he secretly is?)

Chuck Grassley says a few kind words. Later, when "W" is speaking of Grassley, he says something about how he would like Grassley to mow his lawn saying, "He can get the job done for the American people."

Chuck Grassley can mow all of America's lawns? WOW! I wonder what Oliver, of *The Guardian* thinks about that! Grassley must be like the Santa Claus of lawn-mowers, I'm thinkin'. I wonder if he does them all on the same day, like Santa, or if he goes to individual states on a strict schedule. I vaguely remember a television spot Grassley is running now about "visiting every Iowa county all the time." Who knew it was because he was mowing all their lawns? He must be very tired. (I hope he used John Deere equipment; the husband worked there 36 years, and we still have stock.) I thought Grassley used an old folksy car for these marathon trips? Does the old car have a large grass-plow attached to its front bumper? The mind boggles.

Finally, Bush takes the podium. He is introduced by former Mayor of New York, Rudolph Giuliani and "W" says, "Today, the world knows him just simply as Rudy." I immediately think of the movie "Rudy," about the kid who wants to play football as a walk-on at Notre Dame. I wonder if there might be some confusion, internationally, about who we Americans really mean, if we call Rudolph Giuliani "just simply Rudy."

Sean Astin played Daniel "Rudy" Ruettiger in the 1993 film of the same name. It would be really embarrassing to get the two mixed up in public, in, say, England. (Oliver, take note.) Sean Astin went on to play a hobbit with furry feet in "Lord of the Rings." I wonder if Rudy Giuliani has furry feet, like Sean in LOTR. ("Lord of the Rings.")

The only thing I remember about Rudy Giuliani are the details of his messy divorce after he took a mistress. Trust the Super-Moral "Christian" Compassionate Conservatives to have THIS Rudy introducing "W." Seems a bit hypocritical, given the history and all. Maybe, next time, they can get the OTHER "real" Rudy.

There was a REAL Daniel "Rudy" Ruettiger, born in 1948 in Joliet, Illinois,…the inspiration for the movie… who gave us this apropos quote that George W. Bush should take to heart: "Getting what you want is only a problem if you have nowhere to go next." The REAL "Rudy" (Daniel "Rudy" Ruettiger) also said, "Dreaming is a lifetime occupation."

Interesting how these "Rudy" quotes fit the political scene of 2004, because the "good economic news" that George W. Bush now works into his Davenport speech (from here on out) is really dreaming on W's part!

"W" says that "our farmers are making a good living," that he has created 1.8 million new jobs; that the national unemployment rate is 5.4%; that the unemployment rate in Iowa is 4.7%; that "the economy is strong, and it is getting stronger." He says this in the face of the reality being that unemployment really is UP in Iowa.

Ohio has lost 232,100 jobs; Wisconsin has lost 68,000 good manufacturing jobs. Outsourcing of the "good" jobs has doubled over the past 3 years on George W. Bush's watch. If we have 1.8 million new jobs, I'm guessing that every second job he has created requires the job holder to say, "Would you like fries with that? Would you like that Biggie Sized or Super Sized?" I also remember Sally Pederson, Lieutenant Governor of the state of Iowa, at the Jefferson/Jackson dinner in Des Moines, saying that the director of "Field of Dreams" in Dyersville, created more jobs, hiring people to appear in that one

Kevin Costner film, than "W" has created in four years for the entire nation.

But enough about "Rudy," the movie. And why belabor the twisted and just-plain-wrong facts anymore? These poor facts have suffered enough. As have we.

When Bush takes the podium, he repeats much of what he said in his Denver rally, which I attended. Hair jokes (Cheney vs. Edwards). Tort reform jabs (Edwards the target and the scapegoat for all health woes in America.)

Taking a cue from Freshman Rhetoric, "W" announces that his speech has five main parts, or "clear choices," as he calls them:

1) Family security

2) Family budget

3) The quality of life (education, health care; "the soft bigotry of low expectations in our schools," leading to the godawful NCLB (No Child Left Behind) bill.

4) Retirement.

5) The bedrock values of our country which, of course, is a chance to bash the very concept of gay rights, stem cell research, people who aren't Fundamentalist "Christians," environmentalists, et. al.

He originally left out Point Number 4, so bear with me. It was hard for "W" to get it right. It always is.

During the Point #5 portion of Bush's speech, after saying, "I believe that reasonable people can find common ground," he rattles off several outrageous comments, one after another. He says that he "proudly signed the bill" against partial birth abortion(s).

Dr. Howard Dean debunked this "partial birth abortion" misnomer for therapeutic abortions performed in the third trimester way back during the "Sleepless Summer" tour in Iowa. It is a Republican trick; don't fall for it. There are no ethical doctors performing "partial birth abortions." Dean actually checked Vermont's records for any during his 8 years in office. Total found: zero. There is no need to tamper with the law of the land on abortion. It stopped many, many deaths from illegal abortions, from 1973 on. If George has his way, women will lose the right to decide about their own reproductive rights. This is the Compassionate "Christian" Conservative way...but it is not the American way. Not for the majority of America, anyway. (*Even truer in the 2012 election, with women's rights under systematic attack, especially those of lower socio-economic status.)

"W" also talks about marriage being "a sacred commitment....a pillar of civilization and I will defend it." This gets applause, although I don't see Mary Cheney, a practicing lesbian, who is in the crowd, applauding. On the topic of the appointment of federal judges, Bush says, "I will move this good-hearted nation towards a culture of life." Girls: if you are of child-bearing age, take note. This is Republican-speak for: "I will roll back Roe v. Wade and make abortion(s) illegal in this country again, if I can pull it off." Just ask the folks at NARAL Pro-Choice America about this. "W" has a few more words about "keeping American families strong," and THEN says, "The job of the American President is to solve problems, not to pass them on to future Presidents and future generations."

I can hardly believe my ears!

I almost can't believe that George W. Bush really realizes what he has just said. The man who has run up a tremendous national debt that our children and grand-children will be paying off for generations and has involved us in a catastrophic war using false data has the gall to talk about "solving problems" rather than creating them, as he has. The man who has pissed off the entire world by alienating nearly all of the civilized AND uncivilized world says this! Then he says presidents shouldn't be "passing problems on to future presidents and generations."

WOW! Hearing that statement at this rally from this pseudo-president is .....surreal! I think I need an aspirin. But I would have to journey to the unflushed rest room for the water to take it. So, no aspirin. I will just tough it out, as I have done for four years under this guy. Besides, health care in this country is pretty questionable, so I had better learn to "tough it out," medically.

The rally ends with Aaron Tippen's song "Stars and Stripes Where Eagles Fly" (I ask a very young teen-aged girl, a C&W fan, who enthusiastically gives me chapter and verse on this song) and, as I exit,

I listen to some middle-aged matrons "tsk-tsking" about Clinton's "morals" and praising Reagan's virtue(s).

I wonder if these ladies remember that Clinton has remained married to Hilary ("for richer for poorer, for better or worse, till death do us part"), while Ronnie divorced his first wife and family to marry Nancy (or "Mommy," as he called her), who was pregnant before marriage with their first child, daughter Patty. I wonder if the Biblical phrase, "Let he who is without sin amongst you cast the first stone," means anything to them? Or, "Judge not, lest ye, also, be judged."

I realize that, since Reagan's passing is so recent, we must all pay homage to his memory, even though the memory I have of Reagan is that he ran up a HUGE debt (sound familiar?) and began to "lose it," mentally, before he was out of office. [Not that I hold THAT against him: my own dear father had Alzheimer's disease at the end.]

Degenerative Alzheimer's disease is a tough thing to watch progress in your loved one. If stem cell researchers were turned loose with ALL the strains of stem cells that "W" has restricted access to, we might be able to cure that disease and many, many others. Still, when the person "losing it," mentally, is the Leader of the Free World, and it's happening before your very eyes on national television (as it did), it gives one pause. "Let me just say this about that." (Name the President.) Let's be gracious here: some credit Reagan for the collapse of Communist Russia…although that is debatable.

I am extremely happy to add this late-breaking news release from the Kerry/Edwards campaign headquarters. Within 100 days of taking office, John Kerry and John Edwards will hold a "rural summit" meeting in Ames, Iowa, to discuss the problems of Midwesterners. "They will immediately end tax incentives to ship good jobs overseas and, instead, give tax breaks to companies who create jobs here in America."

Put my vote down for the ideas in that last paragraph, lighten up on the C&W soaring and flying and tube-sinking, and PLEASE, PLEASE: Republican ladies: FLUSH when you're done in the rest room. (Gack.) I know you were raised better than that in those compassionate conservative households!

(*That last has been a public service announcement; it does not necessarily represent the view of www.blogforiowa.com. Although it should.)

Correction

The very nice Oliver from "The Guardian" corresponded with me to let me know that the "LaCrosse" mentioned in my report from the Bush rally in Davenport, Iowa, on Monday, October 25, (copy of which I sent him) was LaCrosse, Wisconsin, not LaCrosse, the sport. I regret the error and tell all readers to forgetaboutit, as far as foreign visitors leaving Iowa thinking that we all play some strange game with a little stick with a basket attached to it as a way to pass the time.

Oliver did not say what he thought of LaCrosse, Wisconsin, but I'll bet that, since he is assigned to attending only the Republican rallies, while someone else gets to go to the Democratic rallies, that right about now he is thinking about taking up LaCrosse, the sport, just to relieve the tedium.

White House Press Corps Member: Part One

September 14th, 2004 Denver, Colorado...

AND YOU ARE THERE!

Whatever made me think that I could masquerade as a good Republican and get a White House Press Pass for the Bush Rally at Coors Amphitheatre in Denver, Colorado, on Tuesday, September 14th, 2004? I do own a "good Republican cloth coat," but it was much too warm for wearing it.

So I put on my best Omega gold jewelry and my caramel-colored Jones of New York three-piece suit with matching heels to pick up my tickets. The woman making us sign our names, addresses and serial numbers complimented me on my outfit. I was, as they say, "In like Flynn." (Or was it Flint?) I brazenly asked her, "How do I go about getting a Press Pass for the event?" Here comes, as Paul Harvey used to say, "The rest of the story."

As it turned out, it was no easy matter getting this official White House Press Pass. You had to fax a request, on letterhead, complete with your name, date of birth, social security number, organization for which you wrote, your affiliation with this organization, your blood type and your approximate net worth. I'm just kidding about the last two, but I'm not kidding about the others. [And me without a letterhead! Or enough net worth!]

My trusty Republican friend, Sue Ann, and I had just returned from my book signing, in the scenic prison town of Canon City (7 miles from the Royal Gorge). It was midnight. We had to gerry rig a "letterhead" from the blog picture, provide the information requested, and fax it. We also had phone numbers to call, which I did at 6 a.m. the day of the event (no answers). It was midnight, the night before the event.

"But they won't get this until the day of the event," said Sue Ann.

I fixed her with a steely gaze. "That's the beauty part, Sue Ann. It's genius!

I'm counting on it, in fact…That, plus your vast array of camera equipment. Hang everything you own around your neck! We'll either look very official or we'll look like lost Japanese tourists."

We were told not to bring purses, but to bring cameras. When we got to Fiddlar's Green (as it was once known) before 8 a.m., as required, big signs said, "NO CAMERAS. NO PURSES. NO CELL PHONES." Women were scurrying back to their suburban matron SUV's to leave unwanted items.

We had taken cameras aplenty, cell phones aplenty, a notebook (in my case), and the Kerry/Edwards media passes I had secured in Des Moines, plus a copy of the Midnight Missive with our Blog for Iowa logo. [I don't want to disappoint our faithful readers, but they obviously did not know what Blog for Iowa is.]

"Which way is the Press entrance?" we politely asked the first officer we saw directing traffic.

At Checkpoint Charlie, the young man on the cell phone said, "Where are your Press Passes?" I explained that we had just reached town last night at midnight (true) and that we had faxed in our permission to attend (also true). I mentioned the book tour through Colorado and the fact that I did not know that Bush would be holding a rally while I was in town (ALSO true.) I did not mention anything else. Ever.

"Where are your credentials from your last event?"

I produced the Kerry/Edwards Iowa event Media Pass from my notebook, cringing.

We made it to the next checkpoint, where we went through metal detectors and were "scanned."

Jennifer, of the plunging black dress, irregular hemline, and slingback high heels said, "You'll have to wait here. You're not on our White House approved Press Corps list."

Well, hell no! I wouldn't be showing up on any Republican "approved" lists. Unless it was a list of those most likely to be politely standing there in the approved area next to the boathouse for a peaceful demonstration in Cedar Rapids, only to be pinned to the ground, struggling. My husband made me play golf that Friday and said, "You're lucky I'm making you play golf. Otherwise, they'd be slapping the cuffs on you right about now in Cedar Rapids."

As I lined up to be scanned and searched at the second checkpoint, I was just Middle-aged Midwestern Woman from the Hinterlands, armed only with my Blog for Iowa letterhead, accompanied by a white-haired Episcopalian deacon and wedding photographer, my "publicist." I'm sure we looked very dangerous, indeed.

Sue Ann's deceased mother, Arlene Raymond, my godmother, used to be Mrs. Republican…a lobbyist, in fact, for the chiropractors in the state of Iowa. Hence, Sue Ann had been getting these annoying phone calls about the rally (and hanging up on them) for the five days I had been staying with her. It wasn't until Monday that I had this "Eureka" moment! I had the idea that we could "crash" the party. Sue was not so sure whether (a) we could crash the party or (b) if it was a really good idea to try.

We would soon find out. Bless her heart, she was a trooper!

Since Jennifer had tottered off on her high heels to seek further approval(s), I asked her, just before she departed, if I could go to the bathroom while I waited, a rest room evident just to the left of the metal detector entrance. Jennifer seemed unsure if she should allow me,.... a woman old enough to be her mother, to urinate,... a natural bodily function. She hesitated and then said, "Well.......ok." I guess Republicans never go. Did they think I was going to assemble a nuclear bomb in the Women's Rest Room in five minutes? Did I really appear to be that nefarious? Me...who can barely work the microwave?

Did I look that dangerous, dancing around in the "hold-it-in" elementary school dance, that letting me out of her sight was dicey, or was Jennifer just drunk with power? Fortunately, I did not really care if she said "yes" or "no," as I had drunk three cans of Diet Dr. Pepper (with caffeine) at the crack of dawn in an attempt to wake up and was fast becoming someone who needed to find a bathroom pronto. I was not going to give the Republicans the satisfaction of wetting my pants before the event.

When Jennifer teetered back into view, she led us to the Press Area which was approximately mid-Arena at the Coors Amphitheatre. Sue Ann assumed her position on the risers, enduring some abuse from other photographers for her late entry. I took up a position just below, next to the Channel 4 anchorman, as it turned out, who acted very blasé and whose only notes on the speech were "40 minutes." (I peeked.)

White House Press Corps Member: Part Two

When last we left Connie, she and her Republican ordained deacon/photographer friend, Sue Ann, had finally reached the Press Box at a Bush rally somewhere in Colorado….

There was little happening at first. In fact, the man who came out and slapped the Presidential seal on the podium got a HUGE round of applause, for, basically, nothing. There was a group playing…a local group.

"Do you know any of those people up there?" I asked, repeatedly. And, repeatedly, the answer was, "No." Even I recognized Karl Rove and Karen Hughes when they appeared on a balcony, stage right, but none of the Media seemed to notice. The "staffers" said things in response to my attempts to clarify our entertainment source like, "I don't listen to country music." This from the black-clad Jennifer. For a group that "doesn't listen to country music," the Republicans are sure counting on their votes.[I think you C&W people are being "played." Smarten up!]

Sue Ann and I, both middle-aged and clad in sensible shoes, had warned Jennifer that she would cripple herself before she was thirty if she continued to wear these really high shoes, but she responded, "My grandmother said that, if you want to be beautiful, you have to suffer." (She said this just before falling down four steps. Jennifer has a lot of suffering to go through, from all indications. Just being present at this rally might qualify.)

The types in charge claimed that there were 15,000 present at the rally in the huge arena, which had actual seating. I had brought a blanket to sit on and was using it to conceal a sign (for later) that said, "Bush/Cheney: Farm and Ranch Team." To me, it was a funny slogan, coming, as it does, from the scion of an East coast family with ties to Yale and Saudi Arabian oil. One of the Republicans present, when I wasn't looking, removed the sign from inside my blanket that I was going to take home for my Republican husband and family. Essentially, he stole it from me.

Why does this not surprise me?

An elderly man shouted, "You lied, Mr. President, you lied!" before he was escorted out by an eight-member security team.

The man from KCNC-TV leaned down, at one point, when I sought a seat on the bottom of the camera risers next to the Channel 4 Anchorman and said, "You can't bump those tripods." Well, no, I suppose not. Everybody was guarding their space very territorially. Sue Ann's picture of the sole elderly gentleman protesting was a shot that could have been sold for actual cash. Good-hearted soul that she is, she generously agreed to send it to the professional photographer next to her, who missed the entire fracas, as I almost did, since I was several feet below the riser area. I have a picture of eight men jumping on the geriatric protestor, but it looks like some kind of worshipping of the Sun God, as I was shooting into the sun and got only their backs. They must have felt very brave, subduing a man who looked like he needed a wheelchair.

There were various groups present in the stadium…or, at least, various signs: "Veterans for Bush" looked to be about eighty, both in number and age. There were a lot of "Sportsmen for Bush" signs. This made me think of Howard Dean's endorsement by the NRA and how this might have made him a better anti-Bush candidate, along with his outspoken and unwavering opposition to Bush's war. Later, Dr. Dean would be bashed by Bush, who accused Kerry of adopting the language of "his former rival," that this war was "the wrong war at the wrong time." This was a sign for the crowd to begin shouting "Flip-Flop and waving things back and forth." Pavlov's dogs would have been proud.

John Elway, the Denver Quarterback Hall-of-Famer had been tapped to introduce Bush after Governor Owen finished his remarks on the weather ("300 days of sunshine. Isn't this a glorious Colorado morning?"). Elway read the remarks as though he had just been handed them five minutes prior. So much for Elway's political prowess, unless you consider being inarticulate a pre-requisite for office these days. (And it sometimes seems as though it is getting to be that way, doesn't it?)

Elway: "You must help me re-elect the man who is the ultimate Quarterback leading us all to victory." Well. He's leading us somewhere, all right. And he's the ultimate something. Reminded me of the quote in the Chicago "Tribune" on Thursday from Robert Rudin, former Secretary of the Treasury under Clinton, who said, "In my judgment, we are now on the wrong track on almost all fronts." Since the last Secretary of the Treasury, Paul O'Neill (former head of Alcoa) said almost the same thing in his book "The Price of Loyalty", these sort of simplistic slogans really make you stop and think…(if you are capable of thinking, that is, and not just "sloganeering.")

In 2001, the U.S. was projected to have a $5.6 trillion SURPLUS over the next ten years. Now, in 2004, we are projecting a ten-year DEFICIT of $5.5 trillion, which means that "W" has spent ALL of the surplus that Clinton left this country and again as much in just one short term. And, in 2011, it's $14 trillion of debt. The U.S. debt ceiling was raised 6 times on "W's" watch, 4 times with a Republican majority in control and 2 times with a Democratic majority going along with this disastrous course of action.

So, uh….John…you might want to re-think that statement about where we are being led.

I'm still asking who the band is. Every so often I hear certain words in their song, like "ass." I hear "ass" a lot. One staff member says they are called "Mission Three." Another says they are "Mission Nineteen." I begin to think they are "Plan Nine From Outer Space."

They aren't a bad band; just a bunch of locals, I guess. I try to copy down some of the lyrics I hear, thinking that later, maybe SOMEBODY will have heard of these C&W songs: "Sun coming up over New York City, School bus driver staring at the faces in the rearview mirror. Dreams of fame and fortune." Something about "red, white and blue." OK. Song makes no sense. This is not New York City and I don't see any group waving signs that say, "School bus drivers for Bush." Artist unknown. Heard the word "ass" at least twice. Anybody want to help me out on this one? Certainly supported the candidate well, though, I thought. An incomprehensible country & western song with really crass lyrics that made no sense at all, with references to a city that we are not even in.

O…K. Or, as Jim Carrey would say, "All right-y then!"

Tune in tomorrow, same time, same channel, for the final part of Connie Wilson's adventure through the neo-con looking glass.

When last we left Connie, Bush was just about to ascend the podium. I suppose it will come as no surprise that certain Bush mis-statements cannot stand up to the scrutiny of our Intrepid Reporter!

Bush begins: "Thanks for comin'. I'm proud to be back. It's nice to be out west where the cowboy hats outnumber the ties. And it's nice that the man who led the drive is now out here leading my drive." I assume this is a reference to the almost-inarticulate Elway of the Denver Broncos. It's the "Man of the People" thing, despite the fact that the speaker is anything BUT a "man of the people." Ah, yes, the Good Old Boy network is alive and well.

Bill Owens, the Governor of Colorado, says that we are "safer, stronger and life is better for all Americans," and gets in a plug for Zell Miller, that wacky Democrat. What planet is this man living on?

"W" gets to the real core of his message as to why he should be re-selected, and here it is: "It is most important of all that I be re-elected so that Laura will continue to be the First Lady." It's a variation on the song theme, "Tell Laura I Love Her." To quote the October, 2004, issue of "Mother Jones" magazine (p. 30), "Laura Bush was most famously used to put a friendly face on issues. In April 2001, Laura, the librarian, kicked off the Campaign for America's Libraries. A week later, her husband cut funding for the Library Service and Technology Act, the Reading is Fundamental program, and the National Commission on Libraries and Information Science. Oops."

Bush continues: (he has been thanking everyone in Colorado, individually and personally, for at least 20 minutes, without any substantive policy statements), "I'm a little mad at Ben Nighthorse Campbell (an American Indian senator) for retiring, but I feel a lot better knowing that Pete Coors is gonna' be in the U.S. Senate." Well. That makes one of us. Pete Coors is running ads all over Colorado television making fun of IOWA. Pete Coors, talking about frivolous governmental spending, says, "They allocated (fill in your own figure here) for a rainforest in Iowa. IN IOWA!" He says this last part very sneeringly, as though Iowa is a synonym for excrement. I have a lot of classmates and close friends who left Iowa to teach in Colorado. None of them was amused by this demeaning ad, viewing it as a colossal put-down of our state, (which it is and was.) Keep that in mind if you are a transplanted Colorado resident from Iowa.

I might add, if Coors is so upset over waste in governmental spending, maybe he should read the article "Waste Not, Profit Not" ("Mother Jones", page 23), in which colossal waste is reported by those actually IN Iraq, caused by the sweetheart Halliburton deal. James Warren, a former KBR Convoy Truck Driver says, "The theft was rampant. Most of the stealing was done between 9 p.m. and midnight, when the trucks were at Camp Anaconda. I reported this to my convoy commander, Don Martin, who told me, "Don't worry about it. It's the Army stealing from the Army." (See Joaquin Phoenix 2003 movie "Buffalo Soldiers" for more on this topic, in general).

Warren went on to say, "In March, I called KBR President Randy Harl personally and told him about the theft going on at night at Camp Anaconda. He promised he would get to the bottom of it, and thanked me. I never saw any evidence that KBR tried to stop the theft after my call to Mr. Harl."

Or we might quote Michael West, former labor foreman for Camp Anaconda who said, "Of the 35 or so Halliburton employees at Camp Anaconda, only a handful had anything to do….The human resources supervisor said, 'Don't worry. Just write down 12 hours. Walk around, look around, look busy." Henry S. Bunting, former Procurement Officer, reports that he was requested to break purchase orders down under $2,500 in value, so that "we wouldn't be required to solicit more than one quote. Large requisitions were split into smaller requisitions below the $2,500 level. I questioned this practice early on, but was told by my supervisor to get back to my purchase orders."

So, if Pete Coors wants to worry about "waste," a rain forest in Iowa sounds like a pretty good idea right about now, compared to continuing to support this misguided war.

But I digress.

Bush continues, "With your help, we will carry Colorado again and win a great victory in America." After this pronouncement, I called Patrick McKiernan, Press Secretary for Colorado Victory 2004, who said, "This state is dead-even right now. The failed policies of the Bush Administration have lead this country in the wrong direction and the people of Colorado recognize it's time for new leadership and it's time for a change." McKiernan comments that the field staff in Colorado for Kerry/Edwards is "the largest ever seen." I ask how large that is. He says sixty field staffers, commenting, "There are a lot of upset voters in Denver." I ask the logical question, "Well, if this is the largest ever seen, how many have worked for the Democratic ticket in other years?" McKiernan says he doesn't know; he wasn't there. Hmmmmmmm. Ominous.

Now begins the familiar rhetoric (Bush): "I believe that every child can learn and every teacher should teach. I will not settle for the soft bigotry of low expectations."

Well, no, what he WILL settle for is knocking 300,000 more children off child-care assistance under his Administration's new budget, which also freezes funding for Head Start and cuts funding for after-school programs. The Bushies also want to impose new work requirements on families who receive welfare. It is explained, by Frank Luntz, the Republican pollster and spinmeister, that when the Bush team works a room full of women, they say something along these lines, "I want you to tell me what really matters to you. What's your greatest challenge? Because I think I know what it is. Ladies here, I'd say that your lack of free time is one of your greatest challenges." Luntz notes that the "ladies" present are soon nodding their heads in agreement with this, and he goes on to say, "At that moment, you have bonded with those women."

"That's the Bush solution for overstressed working moms. No overtime pay. No child care. No Head Start. No after-school programs. But, hey! At least they're willing to bond!" (page 31, "Mother Jones" October issue.)

Bush is now beginning to talk about Medicare. "We have strengthened Medicare and we're not turning back." Don't get me started. I can't even begin to talk about "No Child Left Behind," as a 35-year educator, or my blood pressure will rise and I'll stroke out (probably the intended result). If I begin examining Bush's position on Medicare or Social Security and how his tax cuts have and will affect it, that will drive me to drink. I don't think I can really discuss this mis-statement in greater detail without damage to my own health, and God forbid that I would need health care in this land at this time.

On to "Dishonesty in the board rooms of America." If I were George W. Bush, I believe, with his close ties to Enron, Ken Lay, etc. I'd just stay away from this topic entirely. Lord knows, it can lead nowhere good for him if you've been reading the papers and have half a brain. Does anyone really believe this man on this issue when he says, "We will not tolerate dishonesty in the board rooms of America?" (I am tempted to put in another "Yeah. Right," but I'm becoming redundant).

The Economy: (Somebody look up the REAL statistics for me, please…the accurate ones.) Bush begins by saying that 1.7 million new jobs have been created since August of 2003. There is no mention of what KIND of jobs we are talking about. My guess: "Do you want fries with that?" My impression: he has the worst record since Hoover and the Great Depression.

Bush also quotes a 5.4% unemployment rate…."lower than the average rate of the 70's, 80's and 90's" and cites, specifically, a 5.1% unemployment rate in Colorado. I had just been at a book signing in a very blue collar town of 12,800 where the prison system is the main employer. The people at the book signing roamed the coffee house/bookstore, but did not buy anything, saying, "I can't afford to buy anything. I just come here, browse the magazines and books for free, and have a cheap cup of coffee. I don't make enough money to buy anything." I believe them. Same way with my junior college students, who were struggling to try to support families and pay college tuition.

We are becoming a very divided society in more ways than one; the rich get richer and the poor…well, the poor just get screwed. No democracy has ever been able to withstand this kind of "class" division, not to mention the Christian Right's ramming their positions on everything else (stem cell research, prayer in the schools, etc.) down our throats. Want a couple of good quotes? How about, "I don't believe there is a separation of church and state." (Tom DeLay) Or, "George Bush was not elected by a majority of the voters. He was appointed by God." (General William Boykin) When the Attorney General spends $8,000 on curtains to cover the "naughty parts" of the statues "Spirit of Justice" and "Majesty of Law," that should tell you something about John Ashcroft.

Had enough? Me, too!

Bush continues to intone: "The economy is strong and we're not turning back." This, of course, gets a huge round of applause, but he quickly leaves the topic to return to the cornerstone of his re-election bid: national security and how he, a draft dodger, and Cheney, another draft dodger (five deferments), are better suited to defend the United

States of America over a man who was decorated under fire and won three Purple Hearts. "My most solemn duty is to protect America. If we show uncertainty and indecision, the world will drift towards tragedy. That is not going to happen on my watch." Interesting. What is it we are "drifting towards" now? The iceberg that sank the Titanic? And, as far as helping make our homeland "safer," I would refer you to Michael Moore's telling interview(s) with the poor guys assigned to police miles and miles of coastland on a budget of about $1.98.

Bush gets personal: "I'm proud of my running mate, Dick Cheney. I admit he doesn't have the waviest hair. I picked him for his judgment, not his hair."

Frankly, Mr. President: I would feel better if you had picked him for his hair. His judgment has been spectacularly wrong and, in one recent mean-spirited speech in Des Moines, which even the staunchly Republican *Wall Street Journal* denounced, he as much as said that terrorists would strike if Kerry/Edwards were elected. Just what we need, our VP suggesting that, if we don't vote for him, we'll all die. (Get your duct tape, folks. I think there's a special on it at K-Mart this week!) Steve Chapman of the Chicago *Tribune* editorial board wrote, on Thursday, September 16th, 2004, "Bush, we are told, is a tough man for tough times. But his record suggests one of two things: Either he isn't that tough (citing numerous screw-ups, such as letting Moqtada Sadr leave Najaf, Iraq, unmolested, with his supporters, to fight again another day) or toughness isn't much of a solution."

Now comes the onslaught: A sampling of some truly outrageous tactics and statements. First, this one:

1) "The American President must be clear in his thinking and must be clear in his speaking in order to effectively lead." (hahahahahahaha) Right after this, I believe he mispronounced both the word "bio-deisel" and the name of the Japanese Prime Minister.

2) "I will never turn over America's national security decisions to other countries." Trust me. No other countries want anything to do with us any more, and most certainly they don't want to be fighting our unnecessary wars. They have problems of their own, and the cost of ours has shown them that this is NOT the way.

3) "Liberty can transform an enemy into an ally." This is a Harry Truman quote. Some nerve. There is no real proof that liberty, alone, has made any country I am aware of our "ally." France has liberty. They used to be our ally. I think the past tense is perhaps the important thing here. Insert your own support for this quote…if you can.

4) "I want a chance for our children and grandchildren to grow up in a more peaceful world." (Certainly why he bombed Iraq back to the Stone Age and is purportedly amassing troops now to move on Iran.) George W. Bush is many things. A president on the side of peace he is not. I just want a chance for my 17-year-old to grow up AT ALL, since we may have to re-institute the draft once "W" really gets rolling on his "Save the World Crusade."

5) "Freedom is powerful." So is money. So is oil. So is the stench of bullshit.

6) "I want to spread freedom to the world, not because it is America's gift to the world, but because freedom is the Almighty God's gift to the world." Careful, George. Some people call him Allah. Some people don't call him at all. Some people would like you to just NOT spread anything you touch in their direction, at this point, because it is all turning to (rhymes with twit).

7) "We will continue to lead the world to make it free and more peaceful." OK. I can't help myself. One more "R-iiiiiiight!"

8) "I will never relent in defending America, whatever it takes." I would reference the previous article on "The Fog of War," and how Castro was prepared to let Cuba be nuked into oblivion. And McNamara's response which was, "Bring down the temple about our heads!"

Robert McNamara, Secretary of Defense under LBJ, found it unthinkable as a strategy that the leader of a country would allow the country to be totally destroyed, just so he could continue on a path of destruction. "W" quotes Kerry, "The whole thing was a complicated matter." Then, by way of retort, he says, "There's nothing complicated about supporting our troops in battle." Uh,…George. We wouldn't BE in battle if you weren't so trigger-happy and bellicose. "Bring it on!" indeed. Any war is complicated. Maybe if you had spent half as much time studying while at Yale as you did on partying and cheerleading and drinking and carousing, you would know this. Wars are very complicated, indeed, and usually dangerous to people and other living things.

9) "We will not stand for the few who would stop the hopes of the many." Nor will the Bushies stand for the many who would (try to) stop the grab for power of the few….their few.

10) "Only four voted for the war and then didn't vote to defend it." This is a slam against Kerry's Iraq position. My feeling: The Johns (Kerry and Edwards) have got to take it to George on the war. Continuing to waffle and not speak out against Iraq is hurting Kerry's campaign. Everyone wants a strong Dean-like voice to say, "This is wrong. Stop it. Get us OUT of there!" The economy. Jobs. Medicare. Bush is killing us on the issue of how only HE, the draft-dodger, and his draft-dodging partner Cheney, can "keep us safe." (Mr. Kerry and Mr. Edwards, if you're reading this: TAKE IT TO BUSH ON THE WAR ISSUE. Thank you. This has been an editorial comment which I felt I needed to say.)

11) "I'm running against a fellow who likes to raise taxes. The rich hire lawyers and accountants for a reason: to stick you with the bill. But I'm not going to let him tax you." (Insert your own gag reflex joke here.) There's that old saying about the pot calling the kettle black, but it would be too much of a cliché to include it, so consider it omitted.)

12) "We've got to stop frivolous law suits that are running up the cost of health care. I don't think you can be pro-doctor, pro-health-care

and pro-trial-lawyer. My opponent made his choice. He put John Edwards on the ticket." There is dirty and then there is dirtier. And then there is dirtiest. To suggest that Edwards and other criminal trial lawyers are the entire reason this country's health care system is in a mess is dirty pool, but you know George. As Pollster Frank Luntz once told Republican members of Congress, "It's almost impossible to go too far when it comes to demonizing lawyers."

13) "My opponent has proposed $1.5 trillion in tax increases. That's a lot, even for a Senator from Massachusetts." Can you say, "Dirtiest"? Nothing like slamming the Kennedys AND Kerry. And the sad thing is: the doctors in this country are buying it, from what I personally have observed. There has never been any love lost between doctors and trial lawyers who sue them. This is W's way to solicit votes on the "tort reform" issue.

14) Bush makes some comments about how home ownership is at an all-time high and follows this with, "Fantastic, isn't it?" (Somebody feed me the real scoop on that). There are many things that are "fantastic." Me being here is really "fantastic." It's like my friends with the questionable marriage who fought all the time. On their 25th anniversary, she sent him a balloon bouquet which noted that they had spent "Twenty-five interesting years together." Didn't say "good," just interesting. If we examine the definition of "fantastic" in Webster's, I agree with the idea that most of the pronouncements I have heard here today are "fantastic." The definition of "fantastic:" bizarre...suggests

that which is extraordinarily fanciful or unreal in design, conception, construction, etc., because of startling incongruities, extreme contrasts, etc. Grotesque: suggests a ludicrously unnatural distortion of the normal or real. Existing in the imagination; imaginary; unreal; grotesque; odd; strange and unusual; extravagant; capricious/eccentric, i.e., "a fantastic plan." Seemingly impossible. Incredible."

So, I do agree that this entire experience has been "fantastic," as defined by Webster's New World College Dictionary (p. 514).

15) "We've got a political plan to help people who are uninsured." No mention of what this plan is or might be. I can imagine how much money Halliburton will make off THIS plan! Not to mention the drug companies. It's government to the highest bidder!

16) "Simplify the tax code. There are over one million words in the tax code." I'll believe this when I see it...ever...from anyone. My husband does taxes for H&R Block.

17) "We open up our markets to foreign markets. I know American workers can compete so long as the rules are fair." (Insert your own joke here, based on recent closings of numerous businesses that are quickly moving the good manufacturing jobs to Mexico and other distant places abroad.)

18) "We must become less dependent on foreign sources of energy." Ask Christine Whitman, former head of the EPA, how far she got saying this sort of thing to President Bush when she was a Cabinet

member. Or Paul O'Neill, who championed the same cause. An oil man says we aren't going to use oil any more. Do you buy this?

19) "I am a strong proponent of America's community colleges. We must expand Pell Grants. We must help more middle income students start their lives with a college education." While a noble goal, costs of college, including junior colleges are rising. There is, however, a concerted effort being made to recruit students from unlikely areas, like prisons, through a variety of area programs with names like the Career Assistance Center. Usually, it is a requirement that no one in the student's family has ever attended college. These students, some of whom have been known to threaten their teachers' lives and who seldom come to class, are worth something like $1400 on the hoof to the college.

The ex-prisoner sits down next to your teen-aged fresh-out-of-high-school naive son or daughter. Neither the professor nor the student seated next to the Time-bomb-waiting-to-go-off knows the history of the individual. Since reading is a problem for these students, an entire cottage industry has grown up of people assigned to read their work to them. These same assigned "helpers" may resort to writing papers for the struggling students, in a misguided effort to "help."

The student then graduates in a field, for example, nursing, unable to read. The potential nurse shows up at the testing center (which I used to run, boys and girls) unable to read. A "reader" has to be assigned to read the test to them. So, you now have a nurse on your floor who cannot read. This seems like a problem, to me, but it does not seem like a problem to George W. Bush, or to Mary T—- who heads up this program, locally, for a large community college. Her response, "Take it up with the legislature." Those, of course, being the people who have voted to fund this effort in the first place.

And so it goes. Colorado retreats into the dimness of memory, and I retreat to my bomb shelter to await the repercussions that may come if we "stay the course" and continue in the direction we are currently heading.

And on that happy note I will leave you to think about how "fantastically" things are going for us under our current Republican administration.

Over and out.

Loss of Cell Phone Can Cause Loss of Mind

The young man on the phone asked for my daughter, with whom I had just been speaking.

Me: "She doesn't live here. She was in college in Nashville and now she is working there. Can I help you?"

Verizon Guy: "Well, I'm from Verizon Wireless. We noticed that she just suspended her service with us, and we wanted to ask her why."

Me: "Well, you should really be asking me. I'm the one who paid her phone bills all these years until she graduated on August 14th. What's your question?"

Verizon Guy: "We wanted to know if she was dissatisfied with the service or… Why did she break her contract with us?"

Me: "The service is great. The cost could definitely use some cutting, but the service was fine. She had to quit using Verizon because she is going to be selling Sprint phones, and they frown on their employees using another service, which I'm sure you can understand. In fact, I was hoping that this fact would give her Papal Dispensation to not have to pay the breaking off fee or something…If you want to ask her about her experiences using Verizon over the years, which have been many and varied, including losing 9 cell phones and having her phone taken away twice in high school (service suspended) for failing to maintain a "B" average, I'll be happy to give you her cell phone number. Trust me: it will be either in her hand or at her ear or mouth 90% of the time, so it shouldn't be any problem for her to answer. And, by the way, suspending service is really a pain in the neck. You guys should work on making that an easier process. It works like a charm." (A pause). "I can give you her cell phone number…"

VG: "Oh, we're not allowed to call anyone on their cell phones. If they're driving, they might get in an accident."

Me: "Trust me. I just hung up. She's not driving. She's sitting around at her boyfriend's eating bon bons and waiting for him to get out of the shower so she can take him to work, because his car broke down. Go ahead and call her. I'll give you her number, but I can tell you why she quit Verizon, which, by the way, we are THRILLED about, just THRILLED. Do you know how much money we'll save in just a month? True, she had to pay $140 to get out of her contract, but we'll make that up in one month or less and, from now on, she will have to pay for her own phone bill and, more importantly, her own lost phones."

VG: "Did your daughter have the insurance for lost phones?"

Me: "Yes, she did, but she used it entirely too frequently. Let me run this down for you:

Phone #1: Dropped it in the bathtub.

Phone #2: Dropped it in the toilet.

Phone #3: Dropped it in a swimming pool..

Now it gets more interesting and varied from this point on.

Phone #4: A man at Mother Hubbard's Cupboard in Colona, Illinois called us up late one weekend night. He said, "A gentleman just found your daughter's phone in a ditch outside and brought it in the store and we called the number marked 'home.' My husband went out and picked it up and thanked the kind man. How did her phone get in a ditch outside a Mother Hubbard's Cupboard in Colona, Illinois? Beats the hell out of me!

Phone #5: Left it on the counter at the Coop Tape and Records Store in Iowa City, Iowa during her freshman year in college. That one we got back.

Phone #6: Dropped it in a Porta-Potty at the fairgrounds. (That one we did NOT get back...nor did we WANT it back!)

Phone #7: Was stolen from the glove box of her car while it was sitting, unlocked, in our driveway.

Phone #8: Left it in a cab in Chicago, a cab that drove away. Never got it back, but picture her running after the cab like a dog trying to bite the tires. Called the cab main office. Never saw the phone again.

Phone #9: A bus ran over it in New York City while she was there doing a music business internship. Yes, we had the insurance for lost phones, which we always made her pay herself. Did it help? What do you think?

Now, she does not have the insurance for lost phones because she chose to purchase a used cell phone on Craig's list rather than pay $500 for a new one, but she does get a special employee discount plan. All the years she had her phone with Verizon, the bills were astronomical. It wasn't until quite some time along that we found out we were paying ten cents per text message and she had set the World Speed Record for texting. I swear to heaven, I don't know how that many text messages can be sent in one day. No one at the store ever mentioned that there was a better way to pay for this service, so we just kept getting astronomical bills until my sister-in-law in St. Louis clued me in that there was an "unlimited" option that would help.

However, when Verizon had their Blackberry Storm special, we both got them. This was right after the unfortunate city bus accident in New York City. We both took them back. Neither one of us liked them. I couldn't work it at all. I need a button or a toggle or something. That flat screen was a mystery and who wants all their computer messages scrolled across their phone without a password? Not me, said the Little Red Hen. What's the point of having a password if the cell phone computer messages are just there for the world to read? Kind of defeats the option of password protection on your computer Internet accounts, doesn't it?

My husband and I got the simplest phones you have. I don't text. I don't know how to take a picture with my phone. I can just barely work the message function. Hers? With a little tweaking, we could put her in orbit!

When we found out that she was going to be working for Sprint, we were ecstatic! I said to my spouse, "I'll bet you that we save at least $150 a month on our phone bills now!" My husband doubted my claim. It escalated into one of those old-married-couple fights over who was right. I made him get the bill from last month out. It was over $300. Her share of that bill? $157! So, we are delighted that she is now going to be paying for her own cell phone usage AND her own cell phones, on her own dime. And how much will this service cost her, with the Super Duper phone that sends the Internet to you and all that rot, with Sprint? $35. She just has to hope she doesn't lose Phone #10!

VG: (Suppressed laughter) "What did your daughter say when you asked her about all the lost phones?"

Me: "Well, I have always said she should become an attorney, because she loves to argue. She believes that "the best defense is a good offense." She always tries to "deflect" criticism away from herself by going on the attack and accusing you of something, sometimes something totally unrelated."

VG: "What did you say to that?"

ME: "I said, "yes, I lose things I have NEVER EVER lost a cell phone. Not that I couldn't, but I just never have. Yet, she has lost 9 phones since she began using one at about age 13, at a rate of one lost phone per year. Do you know what she said then,? When I protested that neither her father nor I have ever lost OUR phones?"

She said, "Well, I use my cell phone a lot more than you do."

What's that got to do with LOSING the phone you claim to use more than me? Wouldn't that make you MORE careful about hanging on to it, since it is attached to the end of your arm or ear permanently? Apparently not. See what I mean about how she should go to law school and learn to argue for a living?"

There was a long pause.

Then the Verizon Guy said...

VG: "If she is at her home, could you give me that cell phone number, please?"

Me: "I can and I will. I am delighted that someone other than me is going to have a conversation with her about her cell phone usage. Good luck with that, then."

And I hung up.

R.I.P., Gerard…

And Good Luck Riding Those Harleys to the Funeral

I don't normally repeat stories of "personalities I have known and loved" but I can't help but comment on an obituary that recently appeared in our local paper. It provided much food for thought. I mean no disrespect in my comments. I am apologizing in advance, so you know that someone will take me to task, but remember the names here are fictitious.

I was sorry to see that a former student had passed away at a relatively young age. Defining "relatively" is difficult. For me, it is anything under 100. The former student was 52.

What I remember about this student from my very first year of teaching is that, when I—a brand-new teacher, struggling to come up with creative writing assignments—put 6 possible theme suggestions on the blackboard, taken from a Scholastic Books Teachers' Guidebook I had been given, for the year's first writing assignment, all the possible writing topics incensed the deceased. The young man protested that writing on ANY of these topics was "an invasion of my privacy." Then he marched off to the Principal's office.

The topics in the Scholastic Teachers' Guide included a number of situational ethics ideas, which someone other than me who wrote for Scholastic Books had thought up. The topics seemed to make the student uncomfortable. Here's one example: "If you knew that your best friend had cheated on a test you were both taking, what would you do, if anything?"

There was also the hoary theme assignment (please no "hoary" jokes here), "What did you do over your summer vacation?" I was really struggling and only 21 years old at the time.

But nothing suited the young man who protested the assignment choices by marching to the Principal's office to loudly complain about the theme assignments. I was then, of course, called on the carpet by the administration, although not quite as quickly as today's teachers would be. Now, it is instantaneous to side with Junior and teachers are constantly hauled in to defend anything and everything! In my day (1969-1985) the administration was slightly more supportive. I explained why I had made the assignment and showed the Principal the book from *Scholastic that he had given his first-year teacher to use.* What he said to the student I do not know. Whether the student wrote the paper I do not remember.

My take on this protest, from the vantage point of decades later: said student was trying to get out of writing a paper. Period. He had 6 choices and one of them was as tame as they come, unless he had spent his summer hijacking cars.

What I DO remember about the family and the children I taught (yes, there were 3 of them) is that later, his sister was shot in the butt in a "drive-by shooting" with a pellet gun in a nearby city (okay, it was Rock Island, Illinois)—very late on a Friday night. She was 12 at the time. For that matter, the deceased, "Gerard" as I will call him, was only 13 at the time, and was with her at the time of the shooting. They claimed they were "caught in the crossfire" of a gang-related pellet-gun shooting.

Later, in a MacKenzie Phillips moment, the sister accused her father of incest, but then recanted before the in-house authorities had notified the Department of Child and Family Services. She said she had been grounded and she just wanted to get her father out of the house for the night. These anecdotes may give you an idea of what I was dealing with in trying to teach English to 7th and 8th graders as a first-year teacher. Five of my students were on Death Row when former Governor Ryan abolished it, just before going to jail himself for the drivers' license scandal in Illinois.

But what really struck me about this obituary, which I will reprint pretty much as it appeared, minus the real surnames and some aliases for first names, of course, was something else: "Gerard was a commercial fisherman and had worked construction in the Florida area. He never married. Since he loved living in Florida and all his good friends are here, the family has decided to celebrate his life by riding Harleys to Florida next summer (written in early September) and chartering a boat to scatter his ashes at sea."

Every single member of the immediate family listed had a nickname, duly noted in the obituary. Furthermore, the entire family—men, women and children—are going to drive Harley Davidson motorcycles all the way to Florida from the Midwest for the funeral? Is this a cost-saving measure? No casket, ergo, no funeral fees?

I think of my 92-year-old mother-in-law on the back of a Harley. It just does not seem like a good plan. She fell down last week while walking across her lawn and suffered a concussion. Is everyone in the Vandella family young? I wonder what would happen if my mom or my husband's mom or—perish the thought, me—were to try to get to a family funeral several states away on the back of a Harley, especially one driven by the individuals mentioned in the rest of the article? Would these funeral-goers risk being shot in the butt by a pellet-gun...or worse?

Is it even legal to scatter someone's ashes at sea in this day of "Let's clean up our oceans" and anti-pollution sloganeering? Don't know. Can't tell you. But let's read on, with some of the first names and the last name changed to protect the identity of the bereaved.

"Gerard Vandella, 52, of (fill in your own Florida city here) passed away at Solaris Innovative Hospice Care on (fill in the date of your own choosing.).

Per his request, cremation followed. Amy "Rose" Vandella (sister); Beth "Sissy" Vandella; John "Johnny Boy" Vandella; Kenny "The Hammer" Vandella; Brooklyn "J.K." Vandella; Myrna "Big Momma" Vandella and (my own personal favorite) Judy "Butch" Vandella will ride their Harleys to Florida next summer.

Does anyone wonder why I quit teaching in this district? More importantly, does anyone want to be a fly on the wall when this family group gets on their Harleys, en masse, come spring, and starts the trek to Florida from Illinois? Does anyone, besides me, wonder why they don't ride their motorcycles down there NOW, since it has been unseasonably warm and balmy? Why wait several months? Is the family motto, "Better late than never?"

I know one thing: If I were going to this funeral, I would not want to be riding shotgun with Judy "Butch" Vandella on her Harley.

MOOSEFERATU:

Alternative Titles for the Sarah Palin Documentary

or

"Fear and Loathing in Des Moines"

It was reported in the Chicago Tribune on Thursday, May 26, 2011, that a film about Sarah Palin entitled "The Undefeated" was to be premiered in Pella, Iowa. The Hawkeye state already has a reputation for all things corny, as I well know, being a native, so this seems appropriate.

It seems even more apropos should the Palin person decide to announce she is running for President of the United States, which, as I write this, is still up in the air. After all, if Donald Trump can...and Pat Paulsen before him...why not Sarah Palin? Why else make a movie about a woman who didn't even finish out her full term as Governor of Alaska and is now reported to be buying real estate in Arizona.

The film is a two-hour documentary financed by conservative filmmaker Stephen Bannon. With $1 million and Palin's help and permission, footage has been obtained and included of Ms. Palin's time as a member of the Wasilla City Council. It was not reported if there was film of her resigning her office as governor mid-way through her term.

Besides giving me a heads-up that I must make it a point to catch this no-doubt Oscar-worthy and eminently objective movie, it set off political pundits at the Tribune to the point that an entire article was devoted to possible alternative titles, tongue-in-cheek. They ran in the Sunday, May 29, 2011 Chicago Tribune and, quite frankly, they are too good to keep under wraps. The first thirteen I acknowledge as being the contribution of the anonymous blog posts the Tribune collected. The last twenty-two?

Mine, all mine.

Possible Alternative Titles for the Film About Sarah Palin's Illustrious Political Career

"Mooseferatu"

"To Kill and Field Dress A Mockingbird"

"Children of a Lesser Todd"

"The Devil Wears Mukluks"

"Citizen Vain"

"There Will Be Blood Libel"

"Blazing Prattle"

"Honey, I Exploited the Kids!"

"No Country for Newspaper Reading Sissies"

"Close Encounters of the Third-Rate Kind"

"Nightmare on Elk Street"

"The Dumb Luck Club"

"All About Sarah"

"Dark Victory"

"Forgetting Sarah Palin"

"Children of the Corn Meet Children of the Candidate"

"I Can See Russia from my Seat Ringside at 'Dancing with the Stars'"

"South from Alaska"

"Desperately Seeking Syntax"

"From Within Sight of Russia, With Love"

"The Todd Also Rises"

"Mama Grizzly Dearest"

"Birthers of a Nation"

"Must Hate Wolves"

"Motorcycle Mama"

"Driving Miss Dizzy"

"Death Panel Becomes Her"

"Belfries Are Ringing"

"I Know That You Quit Last Summer"

"Gone Is the Win"

"Dancing Toward the Dark"

"When Sarah Met Romney"

"The Shawshank Refudiation"

"Fear and Loathing in Des Moines"

The End

Well, I can now call myself "a perfect asshole" after completing three procedures to tie off veins in my posterior and "cure" my hemorrhoids. Three out of four Americans have hemorrhoids, according to the good doctor, and more women than men, because women bear children, which tends to make an impact in many ways. Having a 9-lb. baby sitting on your innards for 9 months did not agree with my major organs.

The doctor's office where this mini-surgery was to be performed called me yesterday and wanted to move the final surgery to another time. Why? Because my doctor, "young Dr. Ahbed" (which would be Kiran, who had only been on the job for a couple months when he did my colonoscopy, as I only learned AFTER that procedure) had gone skiing and pulled a Sonny Bono by skiing into a tree and breaking his clavicle.

The office nurse said he would be out for 8 weeks.

I replied that I wanted to be done with this particular surgical adventure sooner, rather than later, and that we were going on vacation, ourselves, in just one week, so could somebody else do it?

They gave me Dr. Gottlieb.

I did not know Dr. Gottlieb, but, since he, too, operates within the Ahbed Clinic (the only place in town that does this particular hemorrhoid banding procedure), I assumed he would be competent to perform what, on two prior visits, had been a very small and not very time-consuming procedure. It feels as though someone has shoved a metal ballpoint pen cylinder up your ass, not to put too fine a point on it.

You felt a cold cylinder thing. You heard a click and you were out of there. And, hopefully, the doctor was out of there, as well. Problems, if any, would occur later, when you might wish to poop. Fortunately, there were no problems with Procedure #2, a smaller vein, but there were a few with Procedure #1.

With Kiran, the clavically-challenged doctor on the case, the entire procedure lasted less than a minute. Although the first and largest vein tied off caused some grief after the surgery, #2 was fine. I expected that #3 (also small) would be a quick and relatively painless procedure with few after-effects. But who really knows?

I didn't know Dr. Gottlieb from a hole-in-the-wall (or an orifice anywhere else.) He turned out to be a rather large, humorless individual who was more-or-less a dead ringer for the stuffy doctor portrayed on "M.A.S.H," Major Charles Winchester. Dr. Gottlieb was not quite as big a person as David Ogden Stiers, (the actor who portrayed Major Charles Winchester in that TV series), but his sense of stuffy pomposity came through loud and clear. I was first led back to lie on a gurney, told to remove my clothing from the waist down, and left there with nothing on from the waist down at 1:45 p.m. on a Wednesday. On the date of my last procedure they told me to get there "before 2" because young Dr. Ahbed was going skiing. I was in and out by 2:15 p.m., that time.

For Vein Number 2, I was in and out faster than shit through a goose, as the clichéd and apropos saying goes. I wasn't in the surgical area for more than 10 minutes total. I barely had time to take off my coat (and pants), the young doctor was in and out, and so was I.

This time, I lay there, reading the magazine I had brought from home. It was very cold in my cubicle. I asked for a second blanket and got one, but it was still cold. Even the nurses agreed that it was cold. One nurse said the air conditioning was running! (It was freezing outside as this was Illinois in late March).

I finally had to get up and get my coat to use as a supplemental blanket. My coat was hanging on the back of a chair in my cubicle. I had received a verbal admonition ("Don't get out of the hospital bed on your own") last time I was here for a colonoscopy, so I had to surreptitiously move to the foot of the gurney, where there is a gap in the sides of the bed, and squeeze through a 2-foot space between the end of the bed's sides and the open foot of the bed. With my luck, had I tried to jump down off the end of the bed, it would flip me into the air like one of those lawn chairs at the swimming pool.

One nurse came back and we chatted a bit about "colonscopies we have known and not loved." I'm bound and determined to have them, as undiscovered colon cancer killed my dad, but these things are no day at the beach. Inexplicably, the nurse left the curtains wide open so that anyone walking by could look in at me, lying there on this gurney with 2 blankets, my winter coat, my *Newsweek* , and the cold plume of my breath above my head, which you could see in the office's frigid temperature.

This constant parade of patients past my open cubicle didn't matter too much after I got my blankets, but there were periods of time when I was mooning the populace, as when I made my escape attempt to secure my coat and convert it to a blanket. The staff didn't seem to care if I was in my little curtained cubicle with the curtains drawn or the curtains open. I listened as they told some hapless teenager in the next cubicle to remove everything "above the waist" (I was wondering what the sex of the individual was) and then forced a tube down the kid's throat. Fun for neither of us. I continued to concentrate on reading about Japanese outsourcing of their Sony brand to China.

Title of that issue of *Newsweek* . "Apocalypse Now." Prophetic.

After lying there for 2 hours reading all of *Newsweek* , Dr. Gottlieb arrived.

I didn't mind waiting for 2 hours, because I had my magazine, but, to break the conversational ice with this doctor (whom I had never met), I made a joke.

"My husband's birthday was Monday and I promised him that, after today, I'll be a perfect asshole."

Dr. Gottlieb looked at me, completely humorlessly and replied, "No comment." (Zero for one).

I tried again, "Well, I know that young Dr. Ahbed is out for 8 weeks, but I just wanted to put this all behind me."

Not even a flicker of a smile.

He then began explaining what he was going to do to my butt.

Since I've already suffered through two-thirds of this 3-visit procedure the explanation was a long time coming. I've been facing my fears and putting them behind me since Pearl Harbor Day. This was the first time any doctor on the case had bothered to tell me what-the-hell was going on, although a nice nurse told me *AFTER* Procedure #1 was complete (but only *AFTER* it was over). She pointed out the veins in one's rectum on a chart and likened them to the numbers 2, 6 and 11 on a clock or some such. To be honest, I was just anxious to put my pants on and leave. But I did glance at the chart and understand that there were 3 veins we were going to "disable," if you will, by somehow tying them off surgically. The veins would give up the ghost and sputter to a grim halt. We'd all be happy and improved and enriched in so many ways.

Dr. Gottlieb put his finger in a surgical glove and shoved said finger up my ass, like a proctology exam that my husband recently underwent. While I didn't think that was a "bad" idea, the young doctor had not done this either time I saw him. [Did this doctor just get off on shoving his finger up strange people's butts, thereby making this the perfect job for him ? And then there was the choking noise of something being rammed down a young person's throat in the next cubicle, so maybe he enjoyed shoving things down people's throats even more? Who knew?]

Dr. Gottlieb then said he was "going to numb it (i.e.. the area of entry) a bit."

This, also, was new, to me, but whatever. He used lydocaine, which I recently got for use in my MOUTH in something called "Miracle Mouth." Another health story for the future. Falling apart at both ends simultaneously.

Now the doctor starts in, telling me how he is going to tie off the vein on the left.

I'm no doctor (or nurse) but I do know left from right.

We had already DONE the vein on the left (Procedure #1) which I quickly said…as did the nurse. I've read that doctors sometimes mark the limb to be amputated with magic marker, so that they don't make this stupid mistake. (*So, I say to myself, if we were amputating a leg, he'd be amputating the wrong one! I wonder how you'd mark a vein inside someone's butt with magic marker. Definitely sounds like an inside job.*).

He now sticks this gun thing, with the banding "loaded" on it, up my butt, and misfires it. Yikes! THAT was an unpleasant sensation and an unwelcome addition to the normal regimen.

"Are you feeling any discomfort?" asks Dr.Gottlieb.

"Well, yes, you just fired something into the wall of my rectum. It's not really the way I was hoping to spend the afternoon, but I think I'll live. There go my hopes for becoming a perfect asshole. Right now, I'll settle for imperfect asshole. Let's just get on with it and do the last one on the far RIGHT." (Can't hurt to remind the doc what-the-hell he's supposed to be operating on, now, can it? I'm just glad I'm still conscious and able to keep him "in the loop.")

"I don't know how this happened, but the little rubber 'bandy' thing fired off the 'gun'-operating instrument that is used and didn't encircle the hemorrhoid at all," says the nurse assistant, somewhat unnecessarily, since I'd already had the thing ricocheting around inside my rectum—an interesting sensation after over 2 hours of waiting for a 10-minute procedure.

Dr. Gottlieb had to withdraw the gun instrument. He and his assisting nurse now had to wait for it to "recharge." If I were a smoker, I would have asked for a blindfold and a last cigarette.

I am beginning to get a very bad feeling about how much this guy actually knows about what he is doing. [Kids: don't try this at home, and don't let people you have never met put strange metal objects up your butt! This means you. Worse, as one of my former seventh grade students found out the hard way when the object shattered, don't stick glass coke bottles up your butt, either. Or gerbils. Or any strange things that you don't know where it's been. Be very careful even giving a stranger access to any of your body's orifices, even if they are supposed to know what they are doing. Keep in mind that you might need to use that opening for something again in the future.]

Dr. Gottlieb now puts MORE lydocaine on my ass and tries again with the "gun." This time, it appears it has worked. Just to make sure, he plunges his gloved finger up my anus for the THIRD time during this procedure, which is three more times than Dr. Ahbed the Younger had ever put his finger up my butt. (Which was none.)

Dr. Gottlieb got off a few comments about the culture of Japan that I barely heard, accompaniment to my *Newsweek* reading, then left, saying, "Have a good day."

The nurse came back and whispered to me, "Dr. Gottlieb likes to use a little lydocaine, so you're going to have a numb butt for a while." The nurse actually leaves me with an entire roll of paper toweling, in case I want to "clean up a bit," which tells you something.

Oh. Great. Just what I was hoping for after 2 hours. A numb butt. Dr. Gottlieb's idea of 'a little' is also different from my own. Made me want to buy stock in the company that makes lydocaine.

I am cautioned about getting off the gurney, due to my tendency to try to escape their clutches at odd moments, evidenced after my colonoscopy of December 7th. Last time I was in for Procedure #2, I barely was left on the gurney long enough to curl up and have this gun thing shoved up my ass, because Dr. Ahbed was in a hurry to go ski into a tree. But the time before that, I had to let myself out and get dressed before the All Clear signal.

The nurse that day was very put out by my take-charge attitude. As I walked to the waiting car after my colonoscopy, she reproachfully insisted on trailing along by my side, as though I would collapse at any moment. The sides are up on both sides of my gurney. It is now 4 p.m. I have been here since 1:45 p.m.

During the procedure, in an attempt to be sympathetic to what must be a scheduling problem created by one of their key doctors being out with an injury for EIGHT WEEKS, and, also, in an attempt to joke around with a doctor who had absolutely no sense of humor, I make a comment about the delays they must be experiencing. As the line in the play "God of Carnage" goes, "I don't have a sense of humor, and I have no intention of acquiring one now." I think Dr. Gottlieb may have written that line.

I say, to the pompous and very stuffy Dr. Gottlieb, "You guys must be really backed up with young Dr. Ahbed out with an injury for 8 weeks. This place is so busy that you should install revolving doors."

Completely missing my intentional use of "backed up," Dr. Gottlieb corrects me, saying, "Oh, he'll be back before then."

Eight weeks is what the nurse told me on the phone just yesterday. Was I lied to? Yet Dr Gottlieb, who has had me lying here waiting for a thirty-second procedure for over 2 full hours tells me there's no delay simply because Kiran's hero was Sonny Bono.

I finally get somebody to put down the side of this hospital bed so that I can get OUT of it without incurring the wrath of the support staff. The nurses are already mad at me for retrieving my coat to keep frostbite from setting in in places where the sun don't shine, but places where you don't usually get frostbite. There is no anesthesia involved in this procedure, so you are not groggy and, really, reading a *Newsweek* for 2 hours while nude from the waist down in a public place that is roughly 32 degrees Fahrenheit is probably enough time for most people. I am good and ready to go. I put on my clothes, take my coat-turned-blanket and put it on (as a coat) and head for the exit.

There is a big sign that says, "Please Check Out Here Before Leaving,"

Two people, one a nurse in green scrubs, one a patient (he was wearing street clothes and had on an ID bracelet) are leaning on the counter where you are supposed to check out. They are chatting about life and when this guy was in last (1988). They are in no hurry. After a long time in line, I'm thinking that the two of them might have been blocking progress at this checkout window *since* 1988.

I stand there, as though waiting in line at the supermarket, only without any progress, for at least 15 minutes. Neither of them moves or seems to finish their "business" (whatever THAT is) or looks behind them to see if they are clogging up the line (they are) or asks me if I need help, nor does anyone on the other side of the counter come to my rescue or act the least bit interested in whether I can get the hell out of there.

I see a woman behind a nearby open office door running some Xerox copies. She looks pleasant. I step out of the permanently stationary line and stick my head in the door and say, "Do you think I can just go?"

She is nice, smiles and says, "What's your last name."

I tell her "Wilson" and leave.

I return home, wondering if I will have any problems ("No shit!") or whether things will be fine, as with Vein Number Two. ("And, folks, behind Vein Number THREE, we have….? What?")

My spouse is in bed, as is often the case in the afternoons with the retired male of the species. He asks how it went. I tell him.

He says, after my last bad experience with the prep for the colonoscopy (which is a story for another day, as it would almost certainly be TMI here), "I'm never going back to that office."

I told him I have now learned the name of the particularly excruciating "prep" colonoscopy procedure that I suffered through on Pearl Harbor Day, the very same evening that Elizabeth Edwards was drifting towards death. It's called "Go Lightly"…as in Holly from "Breakfast at Tiffany's." I quizzed the nurse about why I got this excruciatingly awful prep before my December 7th colonoscopy, which literally left me up all night long, tracking the death of another Elizabeth (Edwards) and drinking enough of this awful stuff to fill a battleship, with orders to get up at 3 a.m. and all sorts of shit (no pun intended) that was very different than any "prep" my spouse or I had ever encountered in our 5 previous colonoscopies. She told me it might be because, when they ask if you ever are constipated, I had answered affirmatively.

Wellllllllllll. I also have "the dreaded wine shits" (also known as the "dreaded rum shits") sometimes, going from one extreme to the other without warning. But I had never been singled out for a "prep" that left me drinking several vats of fluid from a powder in a jug as large as your head. The surgical nurse that day said, "Oh, they gave you the old-fashioned method." I remarked that I never wanted to do that particular preparation again, as, near the end, unable to stomach one cup every 15 minutes, I had stayed up ALL DAMNED NIGHT drinking gallons and gallons of this crap.

For my efforts, I was told by young Dr. Ahbed (the skiing enthusiast) that my preparation was "minimal."

I was also read the riot act by a very peeved nurse, who, after leaving me in the curtained cubicle, alone, for at least 45 minutes, with no call button and no way to summon someone to hand me my glasses and my magazine, I had finally climbed down to get it myself (a no-no, apparently), circumventing the hospital sides of the hospital bed by crawling through at the foot, where there was a gap in the fencing.

Finally, I said, "Screw it!" and put my clothes back on to rejoin my impatient husband, who had been waiting in the lobby for quite some time by then. (Backed up that day, too. Pun intended.)

So, I am home now. I am saddened by the news that Liz Taylor has died today (March 23, 2011). I missed out on a chance to write something about how her death affected me, which would have paid me the princely sum of $15.

Liz, herself, missed out on a major back operation during the last year of her 79th and final year on the planet, when she said, "Thanks, but no thanks" to what would have been something like her 81st surgery. She also insisted on being 15 minutes late to her own funeral in a written directive.

And who can blame her for declining additional surgical attention? Certainly not me, on a day like today.

THE END

About the Author

Connie (Corcoran) Wilson has been writing for publication since age 10 and is the author of Training the Teacher As a Champion (PLS Bookstores); Both Sides Now (humor); Hellfire & Damnation (noir short story collection from Sam's Dot Publishing/The Merry Blacksmith Press, www.HellfireandDamnationtheBook.com); and Volumes I, II and III of Ghostly Tales of Route 66 (www.GhostlyTalesofRoutee66.com) from Quixote Press. She is also the co-author of the novel Out of Time (Lachesis Publishing), www.OutofTimetheNovel.com), It Came from the 70s: From

The Godfather to Apocalypse Now (www.ItCamefromSeventies.com); the children's book The Christmas Cats in Silly Hats and the soon-to-be-published thriller about a paranormal teenager, The Color of Evil.

She was film and book critic for the (Davenport, IA) Quad City Times in the seventies and eighties and taught a film class at Black Hawk Junior College (Moline, Illinois). Connie interviewed local celebrities and wrote humor columns under the title "The Write Stuff" for the (Moline, IL) Dispatch, Metro East and the Rock Island Reminder in the Iowa/Illinois Quad Cities.

Connie has written for 5 newspapers and 8 blogs and taught composition and literature classes at 6 IA/IL college/universities. She currently writes for Associated Content, a 400,000-member blog, which named her its 2008 Content Producer of the Year for her political coverage of the presidential campaign. She covered the 2004 presidential campaign for www.BlogforIowa.com. On March 20, 2011, she was named Midwest Writing Center David R. Collins Writer of the Year.

She is an active voting member of HWA (Horror Writer's Association), IEA/NEA, AWP (American Writing Program), IWPA (Illinois Women's Press Association), and Delta Kappa Gamma Honorary Society for Professional Women Educators. Mrs. Wilson founded and served as CEO of Sylvan Learning Center #3301, established in 1986, and the Prometric Testing Center, founded in 1995, both in Bettendorf, Iowa. Her essay comparing the original "Psycho" to the 1998 shot-by-shot remake ("Psycho Analysis: When Perfect Should Prevail") appears in the Dark Scribes press anthology Butcher Knives & Body Counts and her short stories have appeared in many print and online journals.

Connie holds a Master's degree (+ 30 hours) from the University of Iowa (English and Journalism) and Western Illinois University, with additional study at Berkeley, Northern Illinois University and the University of Chicago. She has interviewed Kurt Vonnegut; David Morrell; Joe Hill; Anne Perry; Frederik Pohl; William F. Nolan and many others for Sci Fi Weekly, Reflection's Edge, the Brutarian, etc., and has won prizes for short fiction from Whim's Place Flash Fiction and, in 2007, from Writer's Digest for her screen treatment of her first novel *Out of Time*. Check www.GhostlyTalesOfRoute66.com, www.OutOfTimeTheNovel.com, www.HellfireAndDamnationTheBook.com and www.ItCameFromTheSeventies.com for information on those books.

Connie writes on a regular basis for www.AssociatedContent.com and www.Yahoo.com and maintains her own blog, www.WeeklyWilson.com.

She can be contacted at www.EINNOC10@Aol.com.

Laughing Through Life

Connie Corcoran Wilson

www.ingramcontent.com/pod-product-compliance
Lightning Source LLC
Chambersburg PA
CBHW060244050426
42448CB00009B/1574